THE KISTE AND OGAN SOCIAL CHANGE

SERIES IN ANTHROPOLOGY

Editors

ROBERT C. KISTE   EUGENE OGAN

University of Minnesota

George Gmelch was raised in San Mateo, California. After
completing his undergraduate studies in anthropology at
Stanford University, he took his graduate training at the
University of California at Santa Barbara where his Ph.D.
in anthropology was awarded in 1974. An athlete as well
as an anthropologist, he played three seasons of professional
baseball in the Detroit Tigers farm system while an undergraduate. Dr. Gmelch spent one year as a research fellow
at the Institute of Social and Economic Research, St.
John's Newfoundland, and he taught for two years at
McGill University before moving to the State University
of New York at Albany where he is an assistant professor
of anthropology. His specializations include urban anthropology, social and cultural change, and Ireland.

THE IRISH TINKERS

 Cummings Publishing Company

The Urbanization of an Itinerant People

GEORGE GMELCH

State University of New York, Albany

Shambaugh Library

Menlo Park, California

307/76
65692

Cover Photo. Tinker family crossing
Dublin to visit relatives.

Cummings Publishing Company, Inc.
2727 Sand Hill Road
Menlo Park, California 94025

Contents

List of Illustrations, vi

Foreword, vii

Acknowledgments, ix

CHAPTER ONE   Introduction, 3

CHAPTER TWO   The Traditional Adaptation, 13

CHAPTER THREE   Rural Exodus and the Urban Environment, 41

CHAPTER FOUR   The Urban Economic Adaptation, 63

CHAPTER FIVE   The Urban Camp: Managing Uncertainty, 91

CHAPTER SIX   Family and Marriage in the City, 113

CHAPTER SEVEN   Settlement, 137

CHAPTER EIGHT   Summary and Conclusions, 157

Bibliography, 165

Index, 175

Illustrations

PHOTOGRAPHS

1. *A tinsmith at work,* 15
2. *A typical rural scene,* 27
3. *Mother and children in a tent on the roadside,* 31
4. *Travellers camped along a side road,* 54
5. *Tinker girls preparing dinner in a roadside camp,* 56
6. *Tinkers camped on a green in Dublin,* 57
7. *Father and son in front of their home in Dublin,* 57
8. *Labre Park, a local authority site in Dublin,* 59
9. *Unloading items collected scavenging,* 67
10. *Unloading scrap at a metal merchant's yard,* 69
11. *Traveller woman selling second-hand clothing,* 76
12. *Traveller girl and child begging,* 77
13. *Close-up of tigins at Avila Park, Dublin,* 93
14. *Shifting to a new camp in Dublin,* 106
15. *Family life at Holylands, Dublin,* 119
16. *Teenage marriage among Holylands families, Dublin,* 129

MAPS

1. *Political Map of Ireland,* 23
2. *Traditional Travel Circuits of Three Families,* 29

Foreword

Dr. George Gmelch's study is the seventh volume in the present series of ethnographic case studies on social and cultural change. No human group today, with the possible exception of a few small populations in the most remote regions of the earth, remains unaffected by other peoples and current world events. The studies comprising this series reflect this basic state of the human condition in the latter part of the twentieth century, and they focus on a common theme: the ways in which members of contemporary societies respond to, and develop strategies for coping with, modifications of their social and/or physical environments. Each study in the series is based on original field research by the author.

Gmelch's study is concerned with the Irish Tinkers, a once itinerant people comparable in many ways to the well-known Gypsies of Europe. For centuries the Tinkers travelled the Irish countryside, and their adaptation to their environment was unique. They had a symbiotic relationship with the settled rural dwellers, performing services for farmers in exchange for food and other items. They were an integral part of rural Ireland, and their social relations with the settled Irish were relatively fixed and unchanging. In the last three decades, however, altered economic conditions affecting most of rural Ireland have brought an abrupt end to the Tinkers' traditional nomadic lifestyle and have forced them to establish semipermanent camps on the fringes of Ireland's cities.

Gmelch's study, we believe, is significant in several ways. His analysis reveals that the Tinkers have successfully employed some of their traditional strategies for gaining a livelihood in their new urban environment. At the same time, the Tinkers have been defined as a "problem" by national and local government and welfare agencies. The urban Irish view the Tinkers as a poverty-stricken people who obviously require assistance and who must be transformed into more "respectable" citizens. As a consequence, welfare measures planned and implemented by others are part of the urban environment with which the Tinkers are now attempting to cope. Gmelch provides a careful analysis of the strategies the Tinkers are developing to adapt to these new forces in their lives and to the uncertainties of the urban setting; he calls our attention to strategies which appear to be adaptive in the short run but can only be destructive over a longer time span. Gmelch goes beyond the details of his own data and suggests some comparisons with other itinerant peoples in Europe and certain populations in America. His study thus has implications for the current debate in anthropology about the validity and usefulness of the "culture of poverty" concept.

This study is a contribution to the anthropology of urbanization, complex societies, poverty, and marginal groups. For students concerned with these topics, other volumes in the present series—notably James Freeman's *Scarcity and Opportunity in an Indian Village*, David Jacobson's *Itinerant Townsmen: Friendship and Social Order in Urban Uganda* and Frank Miller's *Old Villages and a New Town: Industrialization in Mexico*—will be of interest.

University of Minnesota   ROBERT C. KISTE

Minneapolis, Minnesota   EUGENE OGAN

October, 1976   *Series Editors*

Acknowledgments

This book is based on field research conducted in Dublin, Ireland between July 1971 and September 1972, with financial support from the Institute of Social and Economic Research of Memorial University of Newfoundland and from a Patent Fund Grant from the University of California, Santa Barbara. A return trip of four months during the summer of 1975 was made possible by a McGill University Faculty Grant.

I owe many things to many people. Charles Erasmus and Elvin Hatch, my thesis supervisors, gave invaluable advice and encouragement throughout my fieldwork and several drafts of this book. Jim Eder helped me think through the initial organization of my data; Richard Nelson regularly renewed my inspiration to write; Michael Carroll and Bob Kiste offered valuable suggestions on the text; and Joann Somich and Dave Jaeger typed the manuscript.

I am greatly indebted to many people in Ireland. Special thanks are due to Patricia McCarthy, Eithne Russell, Vincent and Margaret Jones, Joe and Betty Barnes, Tom Furey, George Bowles, Victor Bewley, Michael Flynn, Tom Murphy, Joyce Sholdice, and Eilis McCullough—all of whom are involved in itinerant settlement work—for their insights, hospitality and friendship. Pat Langan of the *Irish Times* taught me a great deal about photography which proved useful in my fieldwork. Cyril White at University College, Dublin, helped with my questionnaries, and Sean O'Suilleabhain tracked down important archival materials.

The individual to whom I owe the most is my wife and colleague, Sharon Bohn. She provided moral support in the early stages of fieldwork, when gaining acceptance among the Tinkers was difficult, and she collected a great deal of data, especially on the female side of itinerant life.

This study has also benefited from discussions with David Smith, Judith Okely, Willy Guy, and Hugh Gentleman, my British colleagues who have carried out research among English and Scottish itinerants.

My greatest debt of course is to the Irish Travellers, especially the people of Holylands who not only permitted me to live in their camp and endured my endless questions, but made me feel at home. I am especially grateful to Mick and Katie Connors, Mick and Nan Donoghue, Jim and Biddy Connors, and Nanny Maugham. Without their trust and acceptance this study would have been made much more difficult, if not impossible. Out of respect to individuals who may wish to remain anonymous, all names mentioned in the text are pseudonyms.

State University of
New York, Albany

GEORGE GMELCH

*To Hillary who shared the
bunk in our barrel-top wagon,
and to Fergal and Seymour
who for two years sat on my
desk while I organized my
data and wrote.*

CHAPTER ONE

Introduction

The People and the Problem

Although little is known about them, itinerant, outcast populations exist on the fringe of society in many European nations. In Holland they are called the Woonwagonbewoners, in Norway the Taters, in Sweden the Tattare, in Britain the Travellers, and in Ireland the Tinkers or Travellers. In most cases these people descend from early itinerant tradesmen and peasants who were forced from their lands by famines, war, or poverty. Many intermarried with Romany Gypsies who arrived as migrants from India in Western Europe around the fifteenth century. Today, the distinction between indigenous itinerants and the Gypsies is in many instances obscure, although this is not the case in Ireland where Gypsies were only occasional visitors.

Traditionally, itinerants travelled through rural areas performing a variety of trades and services, including tinsmithing, peddling, horse dealing, and seasonal farm labor. Most travelled regular circuits within a relatively small area of the countryside, camping in tents and wagons on the outskirts of the towns and villages they sought work in. In recent decades, modernization has eliminated the need for many of their traditional skills and with it much of the basis of their rural, nomadic way of life. Most itinerants have been forced to migrate to urban areas in search of new sources of income, and this change has had important consequences on other areas of their lives.

This book concerns one such group—the Irish Tinkers.[1]
Ireland, geographically isolated at the edge of Europe and still
recovering from centuries of domination by the English, did not
begin to industrialize on a large scale until after the Second World
War. Consequently, Tinkers were able to play a useful role in the
rural economy until very recently, and they continue to be one
of the most traditional itinerant groups in Western Europe. As
late as 1961, all but 6 percent of Irish Tinkers were living in tents
and/or horse-drawn wagons (RCI 1963:40). In contrast to other
groups, Ireland's itinerant population has migrated to urban areas
only in the last twenty-five years. And only in the last decade
have significant numbers settled.

The focus of this study is the urbanization of Irish Travellers—
their migration to urban areas and the economic and social adaptations they have made there. Anthropologists first turned their
attention to the processes of urbanization and urban adaptation
in the 1950s, when students of peasant societies began to follow
the movement of their villagers into urban areas and to observe
the changes brought about by the new environment. In some
ways the present study is similar to other urbanization studies.
The rural-to-urban migration of Irish Tinkers resembles that of
many peasants in that both have been forced from rural areas by
the mechanization of agriculture and the resultant unemployment,
while simultaneously being drawn to urban-industrial centers by
new economic opportunities there. But in the urban setting itself the similarity is less pronounced, for unlike many peasant
migrants who settle among urbanites and take wage labor, most
Tinkers remain markedly outside mainstream society, subsisting
primarily on welfare, scavenging, and begging. Like residents of
some Latin American squatter settlements, most Tinkers live in
camps on the outer edges of urban areas, physically separated
from the residential estates of the settled community. Their interaction with settled society continues to be restricted to economic

---

[1]The terms *Tinkers* and *Travellers* are used interchangeably throughout this
book. "Tinkers" is the term used by settled Irish and the name by which
most foreigners know the group. "Travellers" and "Travelling People" are
the terms the people themselves use, and "Itinerants" is the government
designation and the term used by the news media.

dealings—asking for scrap items and alms—and to such formal institutional settings as courts and hospitals. Thus the concern here is not so much with the assimilation of Travellers into urban society, as is often the case in studies of peasant migrants, but primarily with their adaptation to life in large urban camps, at the margins of settled society.

The general frame of reference of this study is ecological, in that cultural behavior is examined as a mechanism for coping with the demands of a changing environment. In other words, culture is viewed as a flexible system of adaptive responses. Here I can do no better than quote John Bennett's description of this research orientation:

> A second meaning of the term ecology emphasizes adaptation or *adaptive behavior.* Here we refer to coping mechanisms or a way of dealing with people and resources in order to attain goals and solve problems. Our emphasis here is not on relationships between institutions, groups or aggregates of data, but on patterns of behavior: problem-solving, decision making, consuming or not consuming, inventing, innovating, migrating, staying (Bennett 1969:11).

Most anthropological studies of adaptation focul first on the interrelationship between a group's technology and the physical environment, and second on the behavior patterns required in the exploitation of the environment. Meggars (1971), for example, describes how two different Amazon environments affect the population size, marriage patterns, and other socioeconomic aspects of local Indian cultures. A fundamental difference between the present ecological study of adaptation and most others is that Irish Tinkers represent a population which has always adapted more to a social environment than to a physical one. As itinerants, they were dependent not so much on the wild plants and game of the natural environment as on the resources of the rural farming population who provided them with their subsistence (farm produce, second-hand clothing, and cash) in exchange for labor and services. Thus Tinkers originally adapted to the needs of individual farmers and to the agricultural cycle. Today they have adjusted their life to the urban house-dwelling population, especially to the housewives and charities who give them alms and scrap items and who purchase the things they sell. The resources Travellers exploit are not natural ones but what Bennett (1969) refers to as "social resources." Travellers develop strategies to exploit the social resources of the settled Irish just as hunter-gatherers develop strategies to exploit the natural resources of their physical environment.

A major advantage of an ecological approach in the study of an economically marginal and socially outcast group such as the Tinkers is that it provides a framework for understanding how certain behavior patterns, which might appear pathological or dysfunctional, in fact have adaptive significance. Eames and Goode (1973) have demonstrated that many behavior patterns of the poor are "coping responses," designed to help people deal with the conditions of their poverty. Clearly, however, not all behavior is adaptive: as Valentine (1968) and others have pointed out, some behavior patterns of the poor are merely situationally-specific "reactions" to an environment over which they have no control. Moreover, some strategies which are adaptive in one dimension may be maladaptive in another. For example, such behavior as drinking in response to psychic ills, viewed as "coping" from the short-term perspective of the individual, may be harmful in the long run.

The primary aim of this study, then, is to examine the adaptations of the Tinkers, as both responses to and means of coping with their marginal position in Irish society. Because it is difficult to understand the Tinkers' current adaptation without some background information, the next chapter of this book reconstructs their traditional adaptation to an itinerant mode of life. Chapter Three outlines the factors underlying the collapse of their rural way of life and the resultant migration into urban areas in the 1950s and 1960s. It concludes with a description of their settlement pattern in Dublin, Ireland's largest city. Chapter Four examines the economic adaptation Tinkers have made to the urban environment. It shows how the economic niche of Travellers in the city is structurally similar to their former rural niche and how the exploitative strategies used by urban Travellers are merely modifications of traditional patterns. It notes that one significant change has been their growing dependence on government welfare and on handouts from settled society.

Chapter Five describes the social environment of urban camps. Not only are city camps considerably larger than those in the past, but they often contain unrelated, and therefore rival, kin groups. In this setting there is much distrust, uncertainty, and latent hostility. The mechanisms by which Travellers attempt to cope with these conditions are examined. Chapter Six demonstrates how marriage and family patterns have changed in response to problems created by the social environment of urban camps and the dislocation of traditional economic roles.

In recent years a government-supported Itinerant Settlement Movement has enabled and encouraged many Travellers to settle permanently. Chapter Seven focuses on the reasons many families have chosen to move into conventional housing among the settled community and on the difficulties they tend to encounter in adjusting to settled life. The final chapter draws some conclusions about the nature of the adaptation Tinkers have made (and continue to make) to their changing environment.

The Setting and the Sources of Data

The fieldwork on which this study is based was conducted over a thirteen-month period in 1971-72. A return trip of four months was made in the summer of 1975. The main research setting was a large Tinker encampment on the outskirts of Dublin, about five miles from the city center. The camp, known as "Holylands," was situated on four acres of field set aside for itinerants by the local authority. It consisted of little more than a central field with two strips of blacktop at opposite ends, on which families parked their wagons and trailers and some constructed makeshift huts. Amenities included a single water tap and two rickety outhouses.

During my fieldwork the population averaged eighteen families, whose average length of stay was four months. Six families who had been camped at Holylands almost continuously since it opened in 1969 formed a stable core of residents. The majority of those who camped at Holylands were affiliated with one of three kin groups referred to in this book as the Briens, Driscolls, and McDonaghs.

Residence was maintained for one year in a covered wagon at Holylands. Although my best informants were members of the camp, I gradually acquired a citywide network of contacts by accompanying Holylanders on their frequent visits to other Dublin encampments. Several extended trips were made to provincial towns throughout Ireland to gather information on the adjustment Travellers who had been housed were making to settlement. And one trip was made to Birmingham and Leicester, England to investigate the situation of Irish Tinker emigrants in English cities.

In the field, data were gathered primarily through the standard ethnographic methods of participant observation and directed interviewing. Additionally, two questionnaires were used. In the first, basic demographic information—reproductive rates and family size, age at marriage, and marital residence—was gathered from sixty families. This, coupled with data from the records of local social workers, provided a much-needed statistical profile of the itinerant population of Dublin and enabled me to quantify some of the changes which were occurring in urban marriage and family patterns. The second questionnaire, sent to the chairmen of Ireland's seventy Itinerant Settlement Committees, was designed to elicit a nationwide picture of the Travellers' migration, material conditions, and settlement patterns. In the archives of the Department of Folklore at University College, Dublin, I found information essential in reconstructing the Tinkers' traditional way of life. And finally, the library of the *Irish Times* which had compiled a thick file of all news items on Tinkers since 1960, provided good data on voluntary and government efforts over the years to assist and settle Tinkers.

A Note on the Origins of Tinkers

The key to understanding the origins of the Irish Tinkers lies in the social and economic forces which, over the centuries, have induced Irishmen to adopt a nomadic existence.[2] Many craftsmen were forced to become itinerant when the population in their area and consequently the demand for their skills was not great enough to allow them to remain sedentary. Metal working was one of the earliest itinerant trades, and the name *tinker* was derived from the sound of the craftsman's hammer striking metal.

---

[2] For a detailed discussion of the origins and emergence of Tinkers as an ethnic group, see Gmelch and Gmelch (in press).

As early as the fifth century, smiths travelled the countryside making personal ornaments and weapons in exchange for food and lodging. By 1175, *tinker* and *tynkere* began to appear in written records as trade names or surnames. Other craftsmen and specialists, including tailors, weavers, thatchers, and chimney sweeps, have at various times—especially during periods of economic recession—become nomadic.

Thousands of Irish peasants were also forced into itinerancy through poverty, evictions, and famine. Once on the road, they swelled the ranks of the craftsmen already there. The Irish peasantry, long dominated by English landlords and exploitive economic policies, was one of the poorest in Europe. The lowest stratum of the peasantry—landless "cottiers" and laborers—leased small plots of land barely large enough for a patch of potatoes. Living at the very edge of subsistence, they were especially vulnerable to crop failures, rent increases, and changes in economic policy. For example, large-scale evictions took place in the eighteenth century when many landlords converted their holdings from tillage to pasture in order to take advantage of higher prices being offered on the Continent for wool, mutton, and beef. Thousands of peasants were driven from their lands during the numerous potato famines of the nineteenth century. Unable to afford passage out of the country, and faced with already high unemployment in the towns, some took to the roads to earn a living. Initially they may have travelled only during the summer harvest season, the men working as *spalpeens* (migratory farm laborers) while their wives begged. Without improvement in their condition and lacking opportunities to obtain land, some remained permanently on the road.

A popular belief in Ireland is that Travellers descend primarily from families dispossessed during the Great Famine of 1845-48. This seems unlikely, however, for at the time of the Great Famine the impoverishment of the peasantry, upon whom all itinerants were dependent for their subsistence, was so great that few had food to spare. In fact, more than one million people perished and another million, including some Tinkers, were forced to emigrate.[3]

---

[3] An American folklorist met Irish Tinkers in New York and Massachusetts who had fled Ireland during the Great Famine (Arnold 1898).

Personal problems, such as illegitimacy or alcoholism, sometimes forced an individual or family into itinerancy. The road has always provided an alternative to settled life for those who needed one. The literature contains numerous references to "strolling women"—women stigmatized and driven to begging and sometimes prostitution because of an illegitimate child (Quinn 1966). A severe drinking problem impoverished some families and forced them to give up their homes. In pre-famine Ireland, home brewed whiskey or *poteen* was cheap and enjoyed wide popularity, and the consumption of alcohol among the peasantry was of "gigantic proportions" (Connell 1968).

While thousands of settled Irish were forced onto the road over the centuries, not all became Tinkers or Travellers. Many were able to resettle with the onset of better times, and others emigrated. But those who remained itinerant gradually developed an ethnic identity as Travellers. The basis of their identity was a common adaptation to itinerant life and almost exclusive marriage with other itinerants. There is little doubt that the prejudices and discriminatory practices of settled society against itinerants helped to draw a boundary between the two populations and to foster a sense of oneness among Travellers, arising from their common plight as pariahs. The use of *Shelta* or *Gammon*, an argot spoken only by itinerants, no doubt reinforced the separation. In the last century, their identity as Travellers was further strengthened as they acquired tents and wagons and began camping on the roadside, physically isolated from the settled Irish.

CHAPTER TWO

The Traditional Adaptation

The term *traditional* is used here to refer to the period extending from the mid-1800s until 1950. Much of the following description undoubtedly holds true for earlier periods, but it is only after 1850 that much information on Tinkers is available. After 1950, far-reaching changes occurring in the Irish countryside largely eliminated the itinerants' traditional rural existence. Hence this account is a reconstruction based on a variety of sources, including recollections of the present-day Travellers and settled Irish, newspaper and journal articles, government reports, and archival materials.[1]

The Economy

Unlike the sedentary Irish, Tinkers did not own land from which a subsistence could be extracted, nor did they have an income from steady wage employment. As itinerants they were forced to be flexible and pursue numerous different subsistence

---

[1] A questionnaire sent in 1950 to more than 300 retired public school teachers by the Irish Folklore Commission was an especially useful source. The open-ended questions, which asked the respondents to write as much as they knew, provided information on subsistence, travel patterns, and relations between Tinkers and the settled community. Most respondents had only a superficial knowledge of Travellers, but some knew them quite well and were able to describe aspects of their culture in detail as far back as the turn of the century.

activities. They performed jobs and services for which there was only an occasional or limited demand. A typical village and its surrounding farmland could support a tinsmith, chimneysweep, horse dealer, or peddler for only a few months each year. Because they were mobile, Travellers were not dependent on the market of a single area. Flexibility in the types of work they did was crucial to their adaptation. Since they were dependent upon the peasant population for their livelihood, they adjusted their work patterns to the seasonal agricultural cycle and to the individual needs of each particular farmer they approached. One farmer might need his tin milk cans or stoneware creamers repaired; the next might require help cutting turf or thinning beets. Most itinerants were tradesmen, but they also performed many unskilled tasks in order to meet their subsistence needs.

The primary trade of most Tinkers was tinsmithing. They practiced this craft both in the countryside and in small towns and villages. When working in the countryside, they travelled from farmhouse to farmhouse, often covering many miles a day. The rural settlement pattern in most of Ireland was one of dispersed farmsteads, although small kin clusters or hamlets (*clachans*) of ten to twenty families were common in parts of the West and South until the late nineteenth century (Orme 1970).

Travellers made a variety of tin articles, including cups, kettles, milk pails, lanterns, buckets, and tubs for both domestic and agricultural use. They also made specialized articles upon request. For the children of families living in coastal areas, they made sand pails, for farmers in the West, they made distilling equipment for bootleg whiskey. In 1934 an Irish journalist wrote:

> It is surprising how popular tinware is in rural Ireland. It stands up to plenty of rough usage, and people with big families are generally the best customers of the tinker's tin mugs. The farmers, too, buy tin cans for milking purposes because if a troublesome cow kicks a can the dent is easily removed (McEgill 1934:8).

A large portion of the tinsmiths' time was spent "jobbing" or repairing old tinware. They tightened loose handles, replaced worn-out and rusty bottoms, and plugged leaks with solder aided by a "tinker's dam"—a ring of dough or clay placed around the leak to prevent the molten solder from running off before it

Plate 1.   A tinsmith at work in Galway fashioning a handle for a lantern. Note the handmade tin bucket and milk pail to his left.   *(Photo by author)*

cooled. They also repaired a variety of other items. Many mended umbrellas; some repaired clocks; others, known as "metal-runners," melted bits of iron and cast metal parts such as a new leg for a kettle. Some were skilled at repairing broken china and crockery by drilling small holes in each piece and wiring them back together. In the early spring, before the start of milking season, tinsmiths were especially in demand to repair the large earthenware containers in which milk was separated. They spliced the broken sections together with tin laces which they wove in and out through holes pierced in the earthenware with special drills.

When not seeking jobs in the countryside, Tinkers often worked in the village green. There townspeople purchased new vessels and brought their old tinware to be repaired. Travellers might also obtain sizeable orders from local hardware stores. When the local population had been canvased, usually within a week or two, they moved on. Many Tinkers took pride in their skills, and to this day older men boast about their former work—both about the quality of their goods and the variety of items they could make from a sheet of tin.

From early spring to late autumn, many Travellers dealt in donkeys and horses. Virtually all would swap or sell their animals when an opportunity arose, but some, known as "blockers," were specialists. They supplied many of the heavy workhorses needed for plowing Irish farmlands and the donkeys used daily for pulling milk carts to the creameries. Horse dealers did their best business at the many small county fairs at which horses, donkeys, and other livestock were marketed. Large fairs such as Puck, Bartlemy, Cahirmee, Spancil Hill, and Ballinasloe were known particularly for their horse dealing and for the large attendance of Tinkers.

Travellers acquired a reputation for being skilled horse dealers. Many had an excellent knowledge of horses, particularly when compared to the average farmer, and they drove hard bargains. Part of their success, however, was based on tricking or deceiving buyers into believing that a horse was of better quality—younger or healthier—than it actually was. They used a wide repertoire of tricks: mustard or pepper placed on a horses's rectum irritated the animal, making it appear lively and spirited; a tack driven under an animal's hoof or in its flank, or a dab of arsenic in its food had the same temporary effect; and grooves were sometimes filed in a horse's teeth to make it appear younger. "Knackers"— horses too old and decrepit to be resold—were driven to one of several slaughterhouses and sold by weight. The animals were then butchered and exported to the Continent.

In addition to passing off old, decrepit animals on the gullible, Travellers were also able to trick individuals into selling perfectly healthy animals at low prices by making them appear ill. One informant recalled that he secretly fed a farmer's horse finely chopped chaff. The animal inhaled some of the chaff as it ate; the irritation in its respiratory system created mucus and made the horse cough. The informant claimed to have purchased the animal for half its true value on the following day.

At country fairs Tinkers sometimes acted as intermediaries in the deals of farmers, for which they received a small commission. Known as "guinea hunters," they played a key role in forging an agreement over the distrust and wariness of the seller and the impatience of the buyer. Arensberg and Kimball describe the importance of intermediaries in concluding deals:

> Time and time again he will drag back a buyer who rushes off in well-feigned disgust at an outrageous demand or push forward the hand of a reluctant farmer to be seized by the buyer in the hand-clasp that marks completion of the sale. Amid the encouragements of the bystanders, he repeats the old bargaining cries. He shouts, "Split the difference!" when taking-price and asking-price approach one another, and he wrings concessions from each party until agreement is reached (Arensberg and Kimball 1940:292).

Many itinerants cleaned chimneys. This activity was seasonal; spring and late autumn were the times of year when most people wanted their chimneys swept. Sweeps carried their own tools, consisting of a scraper and a set of detachable rods and brushes. They were paid in cash or produce; their pay depended on the number of tins of soot they collected. One woman described the work of her father:

> Me father had maybe fifty houses in different parts of Westmeath. Most houses needed sweeping twice a year, around Christmas and Easter. The country people kept the work for him every year. He'd sweep the small country cottages during the day, but he had to go early in the morning to the big houses [large estates] to get the job done before the staff had to cook breakfast. They were very big houses with an awful load of chimneys. It was a very dirty job, but there was great pay in it (Nan Donaghue, age 56).

Peddling was an important supplementary source of income at all times of the year. Many Travellers carried a small stock of "waxy" (linoleum), glassware, china, and similar goods on their carts. Most were seconds, remnants, or discontinued stock purchased from wholesalers in the larger provincial towns they passed through. Some goods were acquired in Northern Ireland and smuggled across isolated border roads.[2]   Many of the items

---

[2] Tinkers did a brisk trade in smuggled goods during the Second World War when certain food items, kerosene, tin, and other goods were rationed.

the Travellers peddled were their own handicrafts, including paper
and wooden flowers, reed baskets used for hauling and storing
potatoes, straw brooms, horsehair brushes, wooden clothes pegs,
feather fishing lures, and of course tinware. A Traveller woman
would go from door to door peddling small household wares
from a basket carried over her arm. Shoelaces, needles, scissors,
camphor balls, broadsheet ballads, religious pictures and medals,
and tin cups were popular items.

The Travellers' best customers were the rural farming population, particularly those in remote areas who could not easily
travel to towns to shop. Until this century, shops outside of
provincial towns were few and far between. As a result, peddlers
were important in the distribution of goods in rural areas. And
in an age before the radio and widespread circulation of newspapers, they played an invaluable part in bringing news to remote
areas. Although Travellers generally preferred to sell their goods
for cash, they usually accepted food or second-hand clothing in
payment. Bartering was especially common in the West of
Ireland, where peasants were so impoverished that they had little
or no cash—at least none to spare for such luxury items as a
sheet of linoleum for the living room floor.

During the harvest season many itinerants obtained temporary
wage-labor. In June, farmers with large holdings needed help
harvesting their potatoes and thinning their beet crop; in July it
was hay, and in August oats and rye. Tinkers were often hired
on a contract basis for a stipulated sum per acre or for the entire
job. In this way, they were able to work their own hours and
employ their entire family in the work. Travellers often obtained
odd jobs, such as cutting turf (peat) in the bog and stacking it in
piles to dry. Nanny Nevin recalls her father's work:

> Me dad never was without a few bob [shillings]. If he hadn't it
> in the morning, he'd go up to the farmer's house and he'd ask him
> had they a day's work for him. He'd clean out the out-houses, the
> cow's stable, the pig sty, and he'd go up and make trenches. He'd
> do a bit of cuttin' down hedges right around the farmer's place....
> He'd do his hard day's work and he'd get a few bob, his smoke and
> a good dinner in the farmer's house. Then he'd come down the
> road whistling and singing to the top of his voice, "Are you there,
> Maggie? Here's the money for you now. Go on and get grub for
> yourself."

Tinkers were ideal as seasonal laborers in that they provided their own accommodation, left the area when the work was done, and were unlikely to organize and demand better conditions. But because of mistrust and prejudice, many farmers would hire them only when settled Irish labor was in short supply (R.C.I. 1963:72).

Work of all types for Travellers declined drastically in winter, for this was the season of inactivity on Irish farms.

> It is a period in which all farm work is at a standstill. The farmer has completed the last of his harvest and brought in the last of his potatoes from the field. The cattle are securely housed against the winter cold. The farmer feels himself free to sit round the house during the cold wet days and devote his season to holiday. The working day is at its shortest....It is for him as though the course of the year had stopped and were waiting, gathering its forces for the new year (Arensberg and Kimball 1940:40).

With few farm jobs, little repair work to be done, no chimneys to be swept, and no demand for workhorses, winter was a period of economic scarcity.

Throughout the year Travellers also scavenged; that is, they collected castoffs such as rags, duck and goose down, glass jars, horsehair, and—more recently—old mattresses and scrap metal. When gathered in quantity, these items could be sold to dealers in the provincial towns. Rags, glass, and scrap metal were then recycled; other items were used directly in the manufacture of new products. Horsehair, for example, was used for brushes; down was used in pillows and quilts. But with the exception of down, which fetched a good price, most items yielded only a modest cash income considering the amounts collected.

Begging by Traveller women and children was another important subsistence activity, particularly during winter. Begging invariably accompanied peddling. For some women, peddling was little more than a ploy or excuse to bring the farmwife to the door. If she failed to sell her wares, or even after a sale was made, she appealed urgently for "a bit of help." As one Traveller recalled:

> Once I'd sold some little thing, then I'd start to mooch: 'In the name of God, have you e'er a bit of bread or a cup of milk for me poor childer? God comfort you and may he have mercy on your dead, (Maggie McDonagh, age 50)."

Many women were persistent: once a request for food was met, they might motion to the scantily dressed child in their arms and say, "Maybe you'd have something that would cover this poor creature that the Lord sent into the world." Next they might add, "The other poor creatures below [in camp] are as naked as this one, and maybe if you tried around the house you'd find an old skirt or trouser that you wouldn't want." Travellers were frequently so persistent and presented such a doleful appearance that country people would give them something simply to be rid of them. It was not uncommon for women to curse the occupants if turned away empty-handed: "May you get an angry cancer" or "May the curse of God melt you." Such curses were feared by some but they became so common that the saying "It isn't worth a tinker's curse" came to refer to something insignificant. Many settled folk had their personal favorites among the Travellers who passed through their area and would give to them but not to others.

Some itinerant women told fortunes. Many would simply keep a deck of playing cards lying in their peddling basket in clear view of each farmwife they approached. Their favorite method, however, was "tossing cups"—divining the future from the shapes made by the tea leaves adhering to the bottom and sides of an emptied teacup. Their predictions were invariably of good fortune, since the objective was to place the client in a good frame of mind.

> If I was short of money and maybe I'd have nothin' to sell, I'd go along and ask did they want their fortune told. Well I'd read the cups and tell them all I could. I'd nearly know what to tell them. If it was a young person I'd tell them they were going to be married or they were goin' to get money from friends across the water or they were fallin' into a bit of luck. Anything just to get a livin'. Other Travellers would get a bit of glass and pretend it was a crystal ball. We'd be lookin' through that and we'd tell them to look through it too. Sure, they'd see nothin' and we wouldn't either. We'd only tell them a pack of lies out of it. We didn't care once we got the price of food for our kids. In some houses, with what we'd call a foolish class of people in them, a Traveller could make good money at it (Nan Donaghue, age 56).

The techniques of fortune-telling used by Traveller women are similar to those described for Gypsies (see Clébert 1961). As some present-day Tinkers have suggested, it is possible that the art was copied from Gypsies, who have travelled periodically in Ireland.

Although most food was received in payment for services or given freely, Travellers were sometimes forced to meet their food needs by stealing or poaching. Generally they took only a few potatoes or turnips from the field. But if no one was home, they might take eggs and a chicken or two from the "haggard" (farmyard), as well as clothing from the clothesline. Anything of value that was portable and unguarded was liable to be placed on the cart and taken away (R.C.I. 1963:94). A few women were known to obtain food from farmwives who were alone by threatening them with violence if they did not give; cases of threats actually being carried out, however, are virtually unknown. Occasionally, one Tinker would keep the farmwife busy at the front door, while a companion, often a child, entered the house from the rear and raided the pantry (Sampson 1891). As a rule, however, Travellers did not steal from people they knew or who gave to them generously, and many prided themselves for their honesty.

> I always kept me children in my own place, I never had a woman come to me to chastise me children. To tell the truth, I was very rough with them. They were afraid of their lives. Afraid! Why not? How would I live goin' through the country if they started runnin' away with the people's things? Robbery, that was forbidden altogether. An orchard on the side of a road and a gap goin' in and maybe not a sinner in sight. Well, you wouldn't see one of me children take an apple (Biddy Connors, age 74).

Travellers also exploited a limited range of natural plant and animal resources, although this was considerably less important than their other subsistence activities. During the summer they collected blackberries, billberries, and other wild fruits. They caught fish and hunted rabbits and brown hares. The most common technique of hunting was snaring.

> Long ago me man used to catch a lot of rabbits with snares. He'd be out all night snarin', and you'd hear the rabbits squealing. I

often seen me husband there catchin' twenty rabbits in the one
night. More nights he'd only catch two. And some nights he'd
go where there'd be foxes and all those kinds of big cats and
maybe there'd only be the heads of the rabbits in the snares
(Nanny Nevin, age 50).

Had it not been for the scarcity of mammals in Ireland, Travellers probably would have hunted more. Gypsies in England and
on the Continent, where game was more abundant, exploited a
wider range of fauna, including deer.

Life on the road meant a hand-to-mouth existence for all
itinerants, but living was particularly difficult for those in the
poor and barren West—the counties of the western seaboard, particularly those within the province of Connaught (see Map 1).
The Travellers depended primarily on social resources—jobs, food,
and clothing provided by the settled population—and in the West
of Ireland, people had little to spare. Not only was the soil rocky
and infertile, but agricultural holdings were extremely small. In
1841, 64 percent of the farms in Connaught were smaller than
5 acres, less than half the average farm size in the eastern province
of Leinster. (Despite land reform programs, many western families
still possess little more than subsistance holdings and must depend
on craft industries, remittances from emigrant kinsmen, and outside wage-labor for their cash income.) Consequently, western
farmers had barely enough to meet their own subsistence needs.
As Mick Donaghue recalled:

In the West when you asked for a couple of potatoes, they'd give
you two. In the East they'd give you a bucketful.

Conditions were so poor that many farmers were forced to
utilize some of the same marginal resources as itinerants. Because pasturage was scarce they grazed their animals on the roadside, in direct competition with the Tinkers' horses and donkeys.
Many farmers also snared rabbits; they greatly resented Tinkers
doing the same, especially on private land. To make matters
worse, there were more itinerants in the West than anywhere else
in Ireland. In 1944, when the first census of Travellers was taken,
the ratio of Travellers to settled folk in Connaught was 1 to 365.
The same ratio in the eastern province of Leinster was 1 to 683.

Map 1.   Political map of Ireland

Competition for limited resources required more aggressive economic strategies. Not surprisingly, Traveller women in the West were said to be exceptionally demanding and persistent in their begging. As one countryman recalled, perhaps with some exaggeration:

> The country people never regarded tinkers as objects of charity as they did the poor old beggarmen and women of the old work-house days. These poor creatures begged. The tinkers just demanded and God help anyone who let one of them leave their door empty-handed (I.F.C. 1952a:108).

Travellers from all parts of Ireland were quick to take advantage of house-dwellers when the opportunity arose, but in the West elaborate schemes of fraud were devised. The "gladar box," found primarily in the West, was the best known and most ingenious of these tricks. MacGreine describes how this dummy mold for minting coins was used:

> The "gladar box" is a small box containing on either side a sheet of lead bearing the impress of a coin, generally a florin. On one of the outside edges is a small orifice leading to all intents and purposes to the mold inside. The operator usually approaches a countryman whom he knows to be fond of money, and not adverse to getting it easily. After a lot of beating about the bush he insinuates that it is quite an easy thing to turn a little money into a lot...if one knows how. Provided he is convinced that he has succeeded in creating the proper atmosphere he produces the 'gladar box'. He then proceeds to give a demonstration. He produces a ladle and a quantity of solder. The solder is melted, the 'gladar box' placed on a table, and everything is ready. Lifting the ladle, he prepares to pour the solder into the mold, but—"Get me water to cool the money," he says. While the victim turns to obey, a genuine florin is slipped into the mold and the boiling metal poured into the box. The box is opened and the hot coin falls into the water. Marvelling, the countryman examines the coin. He has already made up his mind to invest some of his earnings. It is not often he gets a chance like this: twenty pounds for five. The tinker takes the money and promises to return on a certain day. He never does (MacGreine 1934:261-2).

Some families were so adept at this trick that they were known by other Travellers as "coiners."

Other European itinerants who occupied the same economic niche as Travellers practiced a similar variety of marginal occupations, changing activities according to local and seasonal demands (cf. Clébert 1961; Heymowski 1969). Of the Norwegian Taters, for example, Barth writes:

> Their livelihood is gleaned from a number of sources: they are tinkers and tinsmiths, they trade horses and watches and various worthless trifles, they beg and occasionally steal, and sometimes take temporary work in roadbuilding or in the winter with their horses they may work in the forests, while the women occasionally work as house-help on the farms (Barth 1955:129).

Shelter and Travel

Prior to the late 1800s, most Tinkers journeyed on foot. They carried their goods on their back or in hand pushcarts. The better-off had donkeys fitted on either sides with *panniers*, a type of wicker basket. They had no shelter of their own; lodging was obtained in hay sheds or in the homes of peasants they met along the way, where they would be given a bed of straw on the kitchen floor. According to Sampson:

> Sometimes a tinker woman, travelling a little in advance of the band, begs a night's lodging at a farm-house under the pretense of being alone. Then, if successful, she hangs out her *patrin* [a sign left on the road to give information to those who are following] and the rest of the band, on their arrival, descend upon the house, which they occupy during their stay in the neighborhood, defying removal. This practice is, however, so well understood in the west and south of Ireland, that tinker women are seldom received as guests (Sampson 1891:205).

But more often, particularly in good weather, they slept on the roadside in the shelter of the hedgerows.

After 1870, the diffusion from England first of the tent and flat cart and later of the canvas-covered "barrel-top" wagon vastly improved the Travellers' shelter and transportation. The first innovation to appear was the tent. According to MacGreine (1934), the tent was introduced in the late 1800s by an Irish Tinker who, after serving a prison term in England, travelled for awhile with English Gypsies and borrowed the idea from them. Their tents were of simple construction. They typically consisted of oil-soaked bags—and later, canvas—draped over hooped willow branches and held down at the edges by large stones. Called "benders," they were semicircular in cross section, from 9 to 12 feet in length and about 5 feet in width. Straw or hay was spread on the floor as a mattress, and heating was provided by a fire, often built within the tent. In 1960, almost 30 percent of the itinerant population was living the year round in tents with no other form of shelter; in 1971, the figure had dropped to 152 families or 12 percent of the population.[3] The horse-drawn two-wheel flat cart, introduced during the same period, greatly increased the Travellers' mobility. Few families had carts before the Boer War (1899-1902), but then many Tinkers joined the army and earned enough money to buy them upon their return to Ireland (MacGreine 1934). With carts, Travellers were no longer forced to walk their rounds, so they could cover more ground and carry a greater variety of goods to peddle.

Barrel-top wagons were introduced into Ireland by Gypsies fleeing conscription in England during World War I.[4] The horse-dealers, who were wealthier than most other Travellers, were the first to acquire them. From Gypsies they also obtained piebald and stewbald (pinto) horses, now the preferred and most common types owned by Tinkers. It was not until the late 1930s, however, that caravans came into wide use. At that time, many Tinkers constructed their own by building a superstructure of hooped timber on the top of their carts, over which waterproof

---

[3]Source for 1960 and 1961 figures for population of itinerants and types of accommodation is the *Report of the Commission on Itinerancy;* 1971 figures are from the Department of Local Government's "Census of Travelers."

[4]Square caravans made entirely of wood were also brought to Ireland by English Gypsies and carnival people, but they were never adopted by Tinkers for several reasons: they were too expensive; they were too heavy for a single horse or pony to pull over hilly country; and their square shape was poorly suited to windy weather.

Plate 2.   A typical rural scene. (*Photo by Pat Langan*)

canvas was tightly drawn. They also contracted carpenters in
various villages to convert carts, drays, and other vehicles into
caravans (McEgill 1934:8). Caravans varied little in size. The
average dimensions were approximately 10 feet long, 6 feet wide,
and 6 feet high inside at the highest point. Inside, benches lined
both walls and a bunk was built across the back. The wagons
were brightly painted and decorated with intricate scrollwork and
drawings of horses and horseshoes. Heat was provided by a small
wood-burning stove. Although caravans offered excellent shelter,
they were not large enough to sleep more than two adults and
several children. Thus most families required both a wagon and
a tent. During the good weather of spring and summer some
Tinkers, preferring the open air and the lighter weight of a cart
which made travel easier in hilly country, swapped their wagons
or stored them with farmers. In 1960, 61 percent of Traveller
families lived in wagons; today the figure is about 15 percent, as
most families now own motor caravans or trailers.

Abandoned farmhouses, known as "waste houses," have

long provided temporary shelter for Travellers during bad weather.

Travellers usually camped along quiet *boreens* or sideroads on the outskirts of towns and villages. The most important factors in selecting a campsite were the availability of water and grazing land for animals and shelter from the elements, usually hedgerows which broke the wind. They returned regularly to the same campsites.

> These camping grounds are constant and are used by all Travellers in turn. You can easily find dozens of them in a day's travel. The blackened circle by the roadside, where the fire had been, the charred sticks, the clippings of tin, the discarded rags in the bushes, all tell their story (MacGreine 1931:172).

MacGreine also described a typical evening in a camp:

> In the evening, when the family have pitched their tent, a fire of sticks is lighted in the front of the tent, and they set about preparing the evening meal. The woman sits in the tent opening, tending the fire, over which hangs a kettle or blackened and battered tin can containing water for the tea. The children sit around and talk and play, while the father reclines in the tent or against the roadside fence, smoking his pipe. Round the fire are scattered various articles, tin pannikins, and perhaps a knife and spoon, the results of the day's foraging, comprising bread, potatoes, a head or two of cabbage, bottles of milk, and maybe a few eggs. The meal finished, the fire is replenished and the children retire to sleep, to be soon followed by their elders, for they usually retire early (MacGreine 1931:172).

Contrary to popular belief and some fictional accounts (such as Stephens 1914; MacMahon 1967) which have portrayed Tinkers as vagabonds wandering the entire country, most actually travelled within a small area. Families usually followed regular routes, seldom covering more than two or three counties. Some particularly horse dealers, travelled wider circuits, the largest of which would include up to ten or twelve counties (R.C.I. 1963:37). Very few travelled all Ireland. This pattern of nomadism within a restricted territory was typical of most European itinerants. Only some groups of Gypsies travelled extensively. The Gypsy *kumpania* (band) that Yoors (1967) lived with, for example, had travelled from their Belgian homeland south to Spain and as far east as Turkey. An early study of Norwegian itinerants notes that one of the major distinctions between the indigenous Taters

Map 2.   Traditional travel circuits of three families

and those of Gypsy origin was that the former were *smavandringer*, or short distance travellers, while the latter were *storvandringer*, or long distance travellers (cited in Heymowski 1969:97).

Map 2 illustrates the traditional travel circuits of three Tinker families. The solid line represents the perimeter or furthest extent of their regular routes. Within this area they might follow many alternate routes. Most families made several complete circuits each year. Travel outside of the circuit did occur, mostly to fairs or funerals, but it was the exception. The circuits lettered *A* and *B* are fairly typical in size of the territory covered by most itinerants; their circumferences are 198 and 230 miles, respectively. Circuit *C*, twice as large as the others, demarcates the route followed by a horse dealing family whose travel was determined by the locations and dates of county fairs.

The average length of stay before moving to a new village or town was about one week. Depending upon a family's reputation and the degree of local prejudice, however, some might be allowed to stay several weeks, while others would be unwelcome as soon as their work was completed. If they were sluggish about leaving or if suspected of trespassing or pilfering farm produce, they would be forced along by the *garda* (police).

In most areas of Ireland, there is a fairly even distribution of small villages and hamlets from 7 to 10 miles apart and of larger towns (population 1000 to 5000) from 20 to 25 miles apart. Thus the distance covered in a single journey between campsites seldom exceeded ten miles.

Itinerants travelled from early spring to late fall while work was available. In winter, during the farmers' slack season and when many of the Travellers' services were not in demand, they moved less frequently. Some took shelter in abandoned farmhouses, and a few built wooden shacks or rented inexpensive accommodation in the slum areas of provincial towns. But most families, especially after the acquisition of tents and wagons, remained on the road the year round.

Social Organization

In Traveller society the nuclear family was, and continues to be, the basic economic and social unit. It was the unit of pro-

Plate 3.   Mother and children in a tent on the roadside. *(Photo by Pat Langan)*

duction and consumption, and except during a crisis such as the illness of the household head, there were no formal patterns of sharing or cooperation between families.

Itinerants typically travelled in groups or bands of two to four families, although families occasionally travelled alone. A basic requirement of itinerant life in Ireland, as well as in most of rural Europe, was that the travel groups be small and widely dispersed. Because they were dependent on the rural farming population, itself dispersed and poor, there were simply not enough social resources in any one location to support a large band of itinerants for any length of time.

Besides increasing competition for limited resources, a large band would create alarm among the local population, who were fearful of poaching, theft, and rowdyism. This in turn would reduce the amount of time the group would be permitted to camp in the area.

> If you were on your own and were quiet and not givin' any of the
> neighbors trouble, you could be there a week or two. But if there
> was a crowd with you, they might give you one night or two before
> you'd have to move along. If you went on your own and not in a
> gang, you may get time to stay . . . it's according to your own behav-
> ior (Mick Donaghue, age 60).

The families who travelled together were generally kinsmen,
most often patrilineally related. They typically consisted of
parents and several married sons; male siblings and their families;
or cousins. Less frequently, unrelated families travelled together.
Personal compatibility, especially of the male household heads,
was an important consideration. If two families met at a county
fair, a pub, or on the road and liked one another, they might
decide to travel together.

The composition of the travel group changed frequently, as
the close proximity and intimacy in which group members lived
invariably gave rise to antagonisms and dissension. As among
hunter-gather bands, conflict was easily resolved by fission: the
aggrieved or unhappy parties simply left the group.

Although no formal kinship organization existed beyond
the family level, Tinkers did recognize membership in a larger
kin group which they referred to as the "clan".[5] By anthropological definition this group more closely resembled a lineage,
in that it included all relatives who traced their descent to a
common, known ancestor, in this case through male links (cf.
Fortes 1953). The term *lineage* is used loosely here, for among
Tinkers it was not a corporate group and had no formal organization. And although Tinkers considered their patrilineal relatives to be the more important, kinsmen connected through the
female or matrilineal side of the family were also recognized.
Because Travellers were mobile and because the lineage was not
a corporate group, a man who did not like his patrilineal kinsmen or who was temporarily alienated from them could affiliate
himself with his mother's or his wife's relatives.

The only occasions at which the lineage—or a large portion
of it—came together were weddings, funerals, and fairs. Funerals

---

[5] The term "clan" is derived from the Gaelic word *clann*, meaning descendants
or offspring.

were particularly important social events. Word of the death of
a kinsman spread quickly, and Travellers often sought the assistance of the police in contacting relatives. Kinsmen came considerable distances and in great numbers to pay their last respects.
After a funeral they often remained camped together for a week,
drinking heavily and enjoying one another's company.

> They'd drink a lot at funerals. Everyone belonging to me would
> drink, because you didn't meet up so often. A funeral was a time
> when all belonging to you would come together in one place
> (Jim Connors, age 76).

The fair, which Tinkers from all over the county and often from
adjacent counties attended, provided the rare occasion on which
members of a lineage might act collectively. At the fair, disputes
between rival groups which may have occurred months before
often escalated into notorious "faction fights" in which lineage-
mates would align themselves against the opposing kin group.
(Such fights were once common among the peasantry as well.)
The fighting, which many fair-goers considered a special treat
to witness, was bloody and sometimes resulted in serious injury.
A schoolteacher wrote of one encounter he witnessed in the
1920s:

> I remember the wholesale use of sticks, stones, soldering irons and
> even iron bars, and the wholesale wounding of men and women whose
> shouts and curses made a bedlam that roused the whole neighborhood.
> Some of the wounds made me shudder in disgust. The injured men
> boasted of their prowess during the battle and the words of encourage-
> ment from their women seemed to placate the pain of their injuries.
> Those who were the best fighters, always the least wounded, hobnobbed
> over pints of stout in one of the local pubs and spoke of the wounds
> they inflicted on their opponents.... In such rows there was much
> blood to be seen and afterwards many bandaged heads and limbs, but
> somehow it struck me that they started such rows to keep up their
> credit in the country and to instill the fear of the Tinker in the
> neighborhood with the usual result of getting a better reception,
> through fear, in their usual daily, weekly or yearly rounds to the
> farmhouses (I.F.C. 1952a:60).

Although Tinkers sometimes claimed to settled Irish that
they were divided into "tribes" and elected their own "kings,"

these were only public fictions, probably intended to enhance
the Traveller mystique.

Little comparable information is available on the social
organization of other European itinerants. Clébert's book *The
Gypsies*, which purports to be a synthesis of the best material
available on Gypsies, does not even hint at the size or structure
of their groups. In the few accounts that do exist, travelling
bands were small, rarely more than three families, and members
were often patrilineally related (Barth 1955; Rehfisch 1958;
Heymowski 1969). Loosely structured and highly flexible lineages similar to those of Irish Tinkers have been described for the
Tater, Gypsy, and Scottish itinerants.

Tinker–Settled Irish Relations

The Tinkers' economic dependence on the settled population
and on manipulative strategies often brought the two groups into
conflict. Aggressive begging, petty theft, and deceptive horse
dealing practices often created antagonism toward itinerants,
especially on the part of farmers. Perhaps the most common
source of friction and complaint was the property damage caused
by trespassing horses and, to a lesser extent, by Travellers themselves. The only grazing legally available to itinerants was the
narrow strip of grass along the roadside known as the "long
acre." Because this land was usually over-grazed or lacked suf-
ficient grass and because animals could easily wander away, Travellers often released their horses into farmers' fields at night to
graze. Besides consuming valuable pasturage, the horses sometimes got into vegetable patches and did considerable damage.
Occasionally, Travellers themselves destroyed property: upon
finding a gate locked, they might break down a portion of the
fence to let their animals in. And when firewood was scarce
or they were unwilling to look for it, they might tear up fence-
posts for fuel. Often the damage was unintentional: for example,
leaving a farmer's storage pit open after stealing a few potatoes
could cause the entire pit to spoil. Nevertheless, itinerants were
blamed for many more crimes than they actually committed.
Whenever something was missing or damaged while Tinkers were

in the area, they were immediately held suspect.

The attitude of the settled community toward Travellers has long been one of suspicion and mistrust. Although settled folk might become fond of certain individuals, they treated Tinkers in general as outcasts. The unwillingness of most to permit itinerants to camp near their community for any length of time is a clear reflection of this antipathy. The following statement by a retired schoolteacher typified the prevailing attitudes among settled Irish.

> They shouldn't be left in a town longer than two or three days. Of course they have to live some place I know, but they should be made to live a certain number of miles from any decent community (I.F.C. 1952b:29).

Many settled folk learned to fear Travellers as children when their parents threatened them, "If you don't behave I'll let the Tinkers take you away." An elderly Traveller recalled the alarm her family's presence struck in settled children.

> Sometimes we'd be goin' along in our pony and car [cart] when we'd come across a bunch of school-children. Well, they'd drop their things and run off like they'd seen the devil himself. I'd get a terrible fright thinkin' one of them might fall and get hurt and we'd get the blame. Somebody must be tellin' them terrible stories about Travellin' People (Biddy Connors, age 74).

Many Irish retained their fear into adulthood. To the present day many avoid walking past Tinker encampments, either by crossing to the far side of the road or by taking a different route altogether, particularly at night.

In the past, Travellers were sometimes harrassed and even physically assaulted by settled people.

> You had to watch yourself when the pubs was closin'. When I heard men comin', I told the childer to 'shush' and put out the candle. Some people would throw stones at the tent if they seen you. One of me relatives in Wexford lost an eye years back. He was sleepin' under his cart not doin' no one no harm when some men came along heavy with drink [drunk] and kicked him in the face (Biddy Connors, age 74).

As the Government Commission on Itinerancy noted, farmers who were irate over Tinkers' trespassing and poaching vegetables sometimes took the law into their own hands.

> Instances of retaliation included assaults on itinerants and attacks on their encampments, seizure of their property, shots fired in the vicinity of camps or trespassing animals, animals wounded or disfigured by various means including slashing, the cutting of horses' tails and manes, and horses being driven long distances (R.C.I. 1963:96).

In 1968, a member of the Irish Parliament was fined twenty pounds for firing his shotgun at a group of Tinkers camped near his home. Despite the ill treatment and prejudice they often encountered, Travellers rarely fought back; instead they packed their carts and wagons and left the district.

Considering the valuable role Tinkers played in the rural economy and their similarity in race and religion to settled Irish—indeed, they are descendants of settled Irish—the discrimination they met seems out of proportion to the petty offenses they committed. Why then were Tinkers treated as outcasts? Part of the problem lies in the very essence of their adaptation: nomadism. As itinerants, they were seldom in one place long enough to get to know the local population. Consequently misconceptions and negative stereotypes about them had little chance of being corrected by close personal contact. It may also be true that the farming population deeply resented their apparent freedom from responsibility and labor. Barth believes that the Gypsies' pariah status in Europe is based largely upon their "violation of Puritan ethics of responsibility, toil and morality" (Barth 1969:38). And among the Norwegian Taters, Jan-Petter Blom notes:

> Within the sedentary population their very nomadism is construed as a denial of the peasant's basic values. As a result they are distrusted, feared, and even persecuted, but they are also admired for their autonomy and recklessness (Blom 1969:84).

In Ireland, as in most peasant societies, land assumed an almost sacred quality, and non-landowners were traditionally denied equal standing by the farming population. Significantly, the itinerant tinsmith was despised while a sedentary tradesman of similar skills, the blacksmith, enjoyed considerable prestige.

Moreover, as many social scientists have pointed out, most societies need a scapegoat—a group upon which the bad luck and frustrations of the dominant group can be directed (Allport 1954; DeVos and Wagastuma 1966). In Ireland, as in many other European nations, the itinerants—highly visible because of their distinctive lifestyle and vulnerable because of their illiteracy and powerlessness—clearly fill this role.

It must be emphasized, however, that relations between Tinkers and settled folk varied considerably. There were many factors involved, including the stereotypes and prejudices of a particular area, the behavior and principal occupation of the Tinkers in that district, the prosperity of the area (where house-dwellers had more to give, the itinerants were less aggressive in their dealings), and even the size of the travel circuit and frequency of visits (families who did not travel widely were better known locally and therefore more likely to be trusted). Local Irish often looked forward to the visits of itinerant families whom they knew well, while despising the less frequent and more predatory visitors.

Tinker's Cant. One mechanism for coping with an uncertain and often hostile social environment was the widespread use of a cant, or secret argot, known as *Gammon* or *Shelta*.[6] Like all cants, its primary function was to conceal communication in the presence of outsiders. Travellers regularly used *Gammon* during economic transactions with settled people. In horse dealing, two Travellers could exchange advice—telling one another what to say or not to say about the animal, what price to offer, when to accept a bid, and so forth—without the farmer understanding

---

[6] Early linguists, notably John Sampson (1891) and Kuno Meyer (1891), believed that the Tinkers' *Shelta* or *Gammon* was the remnants of a "secret language" created before the eleventh century in the early monastic community of Ireland. They speculated that itinerant craftsmen who once worked and resided in the monasteries acquired the argot there. When this relationship between *Shelta* and the early monastic language was hypothesized, the Tinkers were the only known speakers of it. It should be noted that Macalister (1937) and Harper (1971) have raised some doubts about the antiquity of *Shelta*.

what was being said. But perhaps the most important use of *Gammon* was in situations involving threat or danger. At the approach of police, a hostile farmer, or any threatening outsider, a man could secretly warn his companions.

> Travellers use Gammon mostly when there are strangers about. Suppose a policeman came up here and there was somethin' after bein' done, and they were lookin' for some fellow in the camp. Well, once the policeman tells me who he is lookin for I would say to one of the children, "The shadogs are here, tell the feen to clank." The child could carry the message and while the police would be talking to me, the man they wanted would be gone, hid or disappeared (Mick Donaghue, age 60).

Traditionally, Travellers possessed *Gammon* words for most of the principal nouns, pronouns, adjectives, verbs, adverbs, and prepositions; the less important grammatical participles were expressed in English (or, in an earlier period, in Gaelic) or simply omitted. The vocabulary was clearly "copious enough to express all the everyday needs of a material existence" (Sampson 1891: 215). Many of the words and phrases collected by early linguists and folklorists were warnings:

> The shades is toreen, crush! (*The police are coming, get out!*)
>
> Crush out of the gropa! (*Get out of the shop!*)
>
> G'ami luš in that gropa. (*There's bad drink in that shop.*)
>
> I suni the glox of the sārk' tori with his lork. (*I saw the man who owns the field coming in his car.*)
>
> Do the glōkots (*or* šidrugs) misli this tober? (*Do the police travel this road?*)

Other utterances were obviously used in economic transactions with settled people:

> The b'ōr of the k'ena is the glox. (*The woman of the house is the man [boss].*)
>
> What'll I bog for the inox? (*What'll I get for the article?*)
>
> G'ēg a lus from the b'ōr. (*Beg a drink from the woman.*)
>
> Salk (*or* b'ēg) the gored. (*Take the money.*)[7]

---

[7]Phrases were taken from Sampson (1891), MacGreine (1934), and Macalister (1937). The spelling conforms to Macalister.

Although the primary function of a cant was to provide protection from outsiders, some words were incorporated into daily speech even when outsiders were not present.

Travellers still speak Gammon today, and some new words are being created. The size of their vocabulary, however, appears to be much smaller than in the past. The several adults from whom texts were recorded in 1975 had a vocabulary of about one hundred and fifty words.

CHAPTER THREE

Rural Exodus and the
Urban Environment

In the late 1950s, Tinkers began leaving the Irish country-side in large numbers. Forced to seek new subsistence sources as their traditional trades became obsolete, they first migrated to the nearest provincial town or city. A second wave of migration in the mid-1960s eventually brought several hundred families into Dublin, the capital, where they adopted a semi-sedentary existence on the periphery of the city.

This chapter examines both the factors which led to the massive displacement of Travellers from rural to urban areas and the settlement pattern of those now living in Dublin.

In analyzing rural-urban migration, two sets of factors must usually be considered. On the one hand are those internal con-ditions commonly known as "push" factors. These are attributes of the area or community of origin that tend to motivate indi-viduals to migrate. On the other hand are external conditions or "pull" factors: attributes of the area or community of des-tination that attract individuals. Push factors and pull factors are not necessarily of equal strength. In some instances, migra-tion may be precipitated by a single cause such as famine or the exhaustion of a natural resource. For instance, more than one million Irishmen were forced to emigrate from Ireland after the potato crop failed in the mid 1840s. Several factors, both push and pull, induced the urban migration of Travellers in the 1950s, but paramount among them was the obsolescence of the trades and services they had performed.

Collapse of the Subsistence Base

In the decade following World War II, rural Ireland underwent a period of rapid economic change; inevitably, this affected the Travellers, who were economically dependent upon the farming population. First, agriculture became mechanized and production greatly increased. This, together with the reconsolidation of many small and fragmented holdings and generally higher prices for farm products, substantially raised the standard of living of many rural Irish. Country people were now able to acquire new consumer goods, agricultural implements, and the automobile. Improved roads, expanded bus service, and increased automobile use reduced the isolation of rural areas and increased the importance of the provincial towns as marketing and shopping centers. Farm mechanization also sharply decreased the number of jobs available in agriculture—the Republic's major industry—sending many settled Irish to urban areas where employment in manufacturing and commerce industries could be obtained (Meenan 1970). The following pages examine the repercussions these changes had on the Tinkers' traditional subsistence patterns.

Tinsmithing was one of the first occupations to be affected. The introduction of plastic containers, enamelware, and mass-produced tinware reduced the demand for handmade goods. These alternatives were all readily available, and many were cheaper than handmade wares; in the case of plastic and enamelware, the vessels did not rust. Consequently Tinkers were no longer able to peddle the tin vessels they made; nor were repair jobs as numerous, since plastic and enamelware could not be mended.

> We used to deal in buckets and cans and everythin' through the country. It got very bad...they're all usin' plastic now. It's them plastic factories that put down all the tinsmithin'...left Travellers no way of livin' (Jim Connors, age 76).

The demand for tinsmiths declined first in the more prosperous East where new consumer products were first acquired.
As early as 1937, Travellers in County Wexford complained that
new enamel buckets were hurting their trade (Anonymous 1937:4).
By the mid-1950's, tinsmithing had become obsolete throughout
the eastern half of Ireland and survived only in the under-developed
areas of the West. A few Travellers in Connaught can still be seen
making tin vessels at the side of the road, mainly filling small
orders for local hardware stores.

Dealing in workhorses and donkeys declined sharply as farmers
acquired tractors, which were more versatile and efficient than
draft animals. The number of tractors rose from about 4500 in
1946 to just under 40,000 in 1961. By then most of the medium-
sized and large Irish farms had given up animals in favor of machinery. Although tractors were too costly for farmers with small holdings (less than 30 acres) to purchase, it was often possible to borrow
one from a neighbor in exchange for labor. Between 1951 and
1961, the number of horses and ponies used for agricultural purposes dropped by almost 50 percent, from more than 300,000 to
156,000 (S.A. 1969:76). Only in the West, where holdings were
smaller than elsewhere, were horses and donkeys not extensively
replaced by machinery. In that part of the country, horse dealing
remained a viable occupation until the early 1960s.

Not surprisingly, during the 1950s there was a huge surplus
of work-horses. Quick to take advantage of any opportunity, a
few Traveller families were able to compensate for the decline
in dealing by buying unwanted animals at low prices and selling
them to meat packers for slaughter and export to the Continent.
The increase in "knackering," as this practice was known, is clearly
reflected in the number of horses (other than bloodstock) exported,
which more than doubled between 1945 and 1955 to about 30,000
per year.[1] The association of itinerants with this trade led to the
use of the term "knacker" by many settled folk as a pejorative
label for Travellers.

Much of the need for seasonal farm labor was also eliminated
by the introduction of such new agricultural machinery as the

---

[1] Figures provided by the Economic and Social Research Institute of
Ireland, from their "External Trade Statistics."

potato digger and the beet digger. Rural electrification, which
progressed rapidly after World War II, made possible the use of
such important labor-saving devices as electric water pumping
systems and milking machines (Kennedy 1973:96). Between
1946 and 1961, the number of seasonal field laborers in Ireland
declined by 50 percent. Since Travellers were usually the last
to be hired, they were the first to be affected by declining demand
for agricultural labor.

> Not many years ago a Travellin' man could earn a good few bob
> during the summertime workin' on farmers' places—diggin' potatoes,
> pullin beet, and doin' any ole' job. But now its mostly machines
> that's doin' the work . . . there's no need of Travellin' People in
> the country these days (Mick Donaghue, age 60).

A secondary factor in the reduced need for agricultural labor
was a shift in the pattern of land utilization. In the years following World War II the amount of land under tillage was reduced
in favor of livestock production, which requires considerably less
labor.[2] Between 1945 and 1966, the area in tillage declined from
about 2.5 million acres to 1.25 million acres (Meenan 1970:117).

Cutting turf or peat was a common farm job for Travellers.
But even these jobs became scarce. In 1946 *Bord na Mona* (The
Turf Board), a State-sponsored company, began commercial production of turf. It developed machinery which scraped the sur-
face of the bog, macerated it, and then forced it into long sausage-
like strings which were spread in the sun to dry. As a result of
the availability of inexpensive machine-extracted turf and the new
and superior compressed turf briquettes, many farmers abandoned
their own turf production. In the decade after 1954, the output
of turf cut and dried by individuals declined by almost 40 percent
(S.A. 1971). Although hand-won turf production is still the most
practical means of exploiting shallow mountain and western bogs,
the farmers who live in these areas are often financially unable to
hire someone to cut their turf, or prefer to cut it themselves.

---

[2]The amount of farmland in crops has never been more than 21 percent;
in 1970 the figure was just 11 percent. Unlike most of Continental
Europe, Ireland has never been a tillage country (Meenan 1970).

The demand for the small household goods Travellers peddled door-to-door also declined as improved transportation gave country people easier access to shops in provincial towns. This resulted both from the expansion of rural bus service—a program undertaken in the late 1940s by *Coras Iompair Eireann*, Ireland's transport company—and from the increasing number of private cars (Gray 1966:200). Moreover, just as plastics and enamelware replaced the demand for handmade tinware, other inexpensive mass-produced articles reduced the demand for the other handmade crafts the Travellers peddled. The wooden clothes pegs and wood and paper flowers the women once found easy to sell were now replaced by articles made of plastic.

According to Travellers, begging became more difficult as peddling declined. Bartering over goods had often been a prelude to asking for alms, and without this front begging was made more difficult. And although many farmers were now more prosperous, they had less farm produce to give away. When farming solely for their own subsistence, many families had had surpluses of various foodstuffs; but with mechanization and marketing cooperatives, farmers now sold their entire crop for cash. Thus they no longer had the odd bag of potatoes or the extra pint of milk or slab of butter to barter with or to give the Tinkers who came to their door.

A change in the natural environment also undermined the itinerants' rural subsistence base. In the mid-1950s, many owners of large farms deliberately released rabbits infected with myxomatosis in an effort to reduce rabbit damage to their crops. This virus had previously been used to exterminate rabbit populations in Australia and in Europe (Fenner and Ratcliffe 1965). Within a few years the only important animal resource exploited by Travellers became so scarce that most men ceased trapping. Only recently has the rabbit population begun to recover and reoccupy its former range.

Within a fifteen-year period the major trades and services Tinkers performed had become virtually obsolete. The direct causes for their obsolescence—mass production of consumer goods, the widespread introduction of agricultural machinery, improved public transportation, and increased use of the automobile—were external factors over which the itinerant community had no control. Although not all the social resources Travellers depended upon were eliminated—some income could still be earned from begging, odd agricultural jobs, knackering horses, and scavenging— there were obviously not enough economic opportunities to maintain the rural Traveller population at its former level. For the social resources Travellers exploited were not very remunerative: only when taken together did they provide a livlihood. For most families, there was little choice except to leave the countryside.

Urban Migration

Travellers began migrating to nearby urban areas as early as the late 1940s in the East and in the mid-1950s in the West. For this discussion, any settlement with a population in excess of five thousand is considered an urban area. In the 1950s there were approximately thirty such locations, the vast majority of which were regional centers with populations of five to twelve thousand. In most cases the migrants were familiar with these towns, having passed through them on their former travel routes and purchased goods there. Now they camped in these towns, usually along quiet lanes on the outskirts. By 1955 such towns as Mullingar, Taum, and Kilkenny had from twenty to thirty families permanently in residence, whereas a decade earlier they had only sporadic visitors. One informant recalls:

> Years ago us and some of the Joyces was the only Travellin' People stoppin' around the city [of Dublin]. Most Travellers were afeared of it . . . too many strange people and they didn't like driving a pony and cart with all the motorcars on the road. But today things is all turned around. Seems like everybody is shiftin' into the city and no one is left in the country (Mick Donaghue, age 60).

Although the major impetus for urbanization of the Tinkers was the loss of their rural subsistence base, social resources available in urban areas also attracted them. Perhaps the most important of these was Unemployment Assistance, or the "dole." Although the Unemployment Assistance Act of 1933 extended welfare to include persons who had never been employed or "gainfully occupied," most Tinkers were not able to collect as long as they were nomadic, because the money had to be picked up at the same labor exchange each week. To most families in the 1950s, the dole represented a weekly cash income far in excess of what they had previously been able to earn in the countryside. Because only cities and major provincial towns had labor exchanges, many Travellers moved into these areas in order to "sign on" the dole. It was possible to collect the dole at local *garda* (police) stations in smaller towns which did not have a labor exchange, but few Travellers seem to have done this. Their deep-seated distrust of the police and the fact that many small towns were less tolerant of Travellers camping permanently in the area made the larger population centers more attractive.

Since the dole had to be collected in person each week, it was almost impossible for Travellers to follow their regular travel circuits. Unless they had motor transport, which very few could then afford, they had to remain fairly close to town. An individual could transfer to a different labor exchange, but the paperwork involved and the two-to-three-week delay in receiving the first payment made this highly impractical. Thus the collection of Unemployment Assistance not only attracted Tinkers to urban areas but also resulted in a degree of sedentarization by restricting travel.

The availability of scrap metal also drew Tinkers to urban areas. There was never much scrap metal available in the countryside. Travellers earned more from collecting rags, glass jars, feathers, and other discards. But in towns and cities, notably Dublin, scrap metal was plentiful and easy to obtain from construction yards, factories, vacant lots, and dumps. Old bicycles, car batteries, worn-out appliances, and the like could also be acquired from private citizens by going door to door. Because no one had ever collected scrap in this way before, plenty was available. And for the most part, settled people were glad to have it taken away.

In the city it was possible for a Traveller to earn an income from scrap collecting without the labor exchange finding out and reducing Unemployment Assistance payments. Smaller towns did not offer the same degree of anonymity. Equally important, the scrap metal merchants and foundries where Travellers sold their scrap were located in urban areas. Although some scrap could be collected in the countryside, that was less profitable because of transportation costs.

Other attributes of the city also encouraged migration. Travellers found it easier to gain admittance to pubs and cinemas in urban areas where, providing they were not too unkempt, they had a degree of anonymity. In many small towns and villages, on the other hand, Travellers were not served in public places.

Street lighting was another attraction. In the countryside the few street lights were confined to the center of small towns and villages. In urban areas, on the other hand, street lighting often extends to the outskirts of town, providing at least partial illumination for many Tinker camps. When talking about the "old days," adults often mention the loneliness of camping on dark country lanes with only campfire and candle to brighten the night. One change in the life of urban migrants at least partially attributed to street lighting has been their bedtime. Whereas in rural areas most Tinkers retired early, they now stay up late: Holylands children are often up till midnight playing soccer or tossing coins under the light posts.

With each family that migrates, the loneliness and sense of isolation of those who remain in the rural areas increases—and that increases the likelihood that they too will eventually migrate. Moreover, return visits to the country by recent migrants are a strong stimulant for others to move, since at these reunions the migrants exaggerate the profits of begging and scavenging and the amount of charity available in the city. Families often take a bundle of second-hand clothing to give to their rural relatives, claiming that it represents just one day's begging in the city. Because Tinkers are mobile and have no land or fixed interests, many do "shift" to the urban area at the urging of kinsmen.

> First me eldest brother shifted down to Dublin and each time he
> visited us in Wexford he was takin' one of the family back to the
> city with him. Before long all of me six brothers and their families
> was stoppin' in the same green near Dublin. I didn't want to go
> but it's too lonely travellin' by yourself (Patty Brien, age 25).

Although Travellers invariably view their first stay in the city as a trial period, few ever return to their home territory except to visit.

Of course, many settled Irish were also migrating to urban areas—particularly to Dublin—at this time. Between 1951 and

1966, while the population of the entire nation was declining,[3] the number of inhabitants in Dublin increased by 10 percent to 650,000. The increase was due primarily to out-migration from rural areas, especially from the West of Ireland, which lost 17 percent of its population. These figures are not as dramatic as they first seem, however, for they represent but one period in a century-old pattern of rural-to-urban migration and emigration. But the flow of migrants did increase during the 1950s and 1960s, mainly as a result of the declining demand for manpower in agriculture and the expanding employment opportunities in urban industries.

There was no direct connection between the migration of settled folk and that of Travellers, even though the underlying factors causing migration—changes occurring in the Irish economy— were the same. Although itinerants were dependent upon the social resources of the settled community, the decline in the rural population was not great enough in most areas to make any appreciable difference in the Travellers' economy, which was breaking down for the reasons already mentioned. Only in such heavily depopulated parts of western Ireland as County Leitrim, which lost 29 percent of its population between 1951 and 1966, was the decline great enough to affect the itinerant population.

Emigration to England. During the late 1950s and early 1960s, economic opportunities were even greater in England than in Irish towns and cities. The lure of a seemingly endless supply of scrap metal from slum clearance and urban renewal projects (and for some, employment in the construction trades) attracted many Tinkers, particularly to the large industrial cities of Birmingham and Manchester. English welfare benefits, which paid more than those in Ireland, were another incentive. Emigration declined around 1965 as opportunities for Travellers within Ireland improved and as scrap collecting became less profitable in England because of heavy competition and new laws prohibiting the removal of scrap from condemned or demolished buildings. In addition, local authorities in England who objected to itinerants, especially the Irish, squatting on city land took harsh measures

---

[3]The population of Ireland dropped from 2,960,599 in 1951 to 2,884,002 in 1966 (S.A. 1971:20).

against them, including frequent and forceful evictions.[4] Never–
theless, several thousand Irish Tinkers still live and work in England.

Migration to Dublin. The first Tinkers to migrate to Dublin
came from the adjoining counties of Wicklow, Kildare, and Meath.
Like many other Traveller families at the time, they moved to the
nearest urban center to sign on the dole and to collect scrap metal.
Between 1944 and 1956, the number of Travellers in Dublin increased from 38 to 340 (see Table 1). The rate of in-migration then
levelled off, as most Travellers from the surrounding rural districts
had already made the move to urban areas. The 1960 figure shows
only a slight increase in population over the 1956 level, and the
number of Travellers in Dublin the following year actually declined
as many moved on to England to take advantage of the construction

Table 1. Dublin's Tinker Population

Year	Inhabitants
1944	38
1952	158
1956	340
1960	418
1961	258
1971	1,435
1974	2,245

Source: 1944-61 figures from the Commission on Itinerancy (1963:115). 1971
and 1974 figures from the Department of
local Government's "Census of Itinerants."

[4]Local authorities constructed various types of "tinker defenses," including trenches, concrete posts, and piles of earth blocking the entrance to
vacant land to prevent Travellers from camping. Subsequently, some
authorities invaded camps and forcibly towed away the caravans. The
statement of one Birmingham Councillor typified the attitude of some
local authorities: "The Tinker is a throwback to the past and has no
place in the life of a modern city, where people come to live in a settled,
orderly and mutually helpful society. We intend to make conditions so
intolerable, so uncomfortable and so unprofitable for these human scrap
vultures that they won't stop here." (*The Guardian*, 3 July 1963).

boom. A similar pattern of migration occurred in other urban areas: a heavy influx until the late 1950s and then a levelling off.

Around the mid-1960s a new wave of migration occurred in which families from all parts of Ireland moved to Dublin. While the number of Travellers camped around most provincial towns and cities remained stable or declined slightly, the number in Dublin increased an additional 300 percent to 1435 individuals in 1971, or 15 percent of the entire itinerant population. Most of this increase occurred after 1965.

Why did Dublin suddenly attract so many migrants? An important factor was the increased availability of charity from both institutions and individuals. The sudden generosity of Dubliners resulted largely from the publication of the *Report of the Commission on Itinerancy* in 1963 and, more importantly, the work of the first Itinerant Settlement Committee (hereafter referred to as *ISC*) organized in Dublin two years later.

The Government Commission on Itinerancy was established to investigate the problems (trespass, litter, damage caused by untended horses, and so on) created for population centers by the increased numbers of Travellers camped nearby and to seek solutions to these problems. When plans to form such a Commission were first announced by the Parliamentary Secretary, he stressed the government's obligation to protect private property, businesses, and amenities from interference by itinerants. The final report, however, also documented the deplorable state of Ireland's itinerant population—their poverty, unemployment, illiteracy, high rate of infant mortality, and so forth. The Dublin media gave these findings extensive coverage, and many sympathetic editorials began calling upon the settled community to exercise Christian charity toward Tinkers. Soon what was known as the "itinerant problem" became a public disgrace, at least in Dublin.

The Dublin ISC, a private charity organized by a well-known philanthropist and other concerned citizens, took immediate steps to improve the living conditions of Tinkers in the city and to heighten the settled community's awareness of their plight. Toward the first goal it dispensed blankets, tarpaulins, cooking utensils, and twenty wagons, all purchased with money received in donations, to the most needy families. After discovering that some families were exploiting the situation by selling their own tents and wagons in order to receive a handout, the ISC began purchasing second-hand trailers and renting rather than giving them to the families.

Toward the second goal, ISC officials made radio and television appearances to reiterate the findings of the Commission Report, emphasizing the number of families still living under canvas on the roadside and the number of children who died each winter. They explained that once given the same amenities as the settled community, Tinkers would become "respectable" law-abiding citizens. The ISC placed pictures of forlorn, impoverished itinerant children in Dublin papers[5] and proclaimed a yearly "Settlement Week"—a week of intensive publicity and fund-raising activities. Later, it began publication of a bimonthly newsletter known as *Settlement News* to publicize the work of the Settlement Movement, solicit donations, and promote "understanding" toward Travellers. This newsletter and various leaflets were distributed at major public events such as the Dublin Horse Show.

The Commission's Report and the ISC publicity generated great sympathy for Travellers and a desire by many to help. This sentiment was most often expressed through the giving of alms. Begging in Dublin became a lucrative occupation for Tinker women, even more so than the men's scavenging activities. In a single day, a woman might earn as much as three pounds[6] begging on downtown streets; others who went door to door through the suburbs could gather enough food and clothing to provide ably for their large families.

Other factors in the city, such as the greater prosperity of Dubliners compared to country people, also made begging profitable. The high population density of the city enabled women to solicit alms from many people each day. In the words of Nan "the Hand" Driscoll:

---

[5] The frequency with which these pictures appeared finally prompted one reader to write, "Can newspapers never print a picture of a happy Tinker, or is there no such thing? I feel you will encourage more support and sympathy for these Travelling folk if you let people know that they are not always totally miserable." (*Irish Press*, no date)

[6] In 1972, at the time of my original research, one pound (£1) was equivalent to $2.50. For later reference, there are 100 pence to a pound. One shilling is equivalent to five pence.

The houses here is stacked up one against the other. In the country
the houses do be far apart so you can't cover many in a day. But
here it's no bother doin' a hundred.

Many charities which had virtually ignored itinerants in the
past began to open doors to them. The Irish Sisters of Charity
gave bread each day, and St. Vincent de Paul Societies distributed
clothing. There were also the goods and trailers the Dublin ISC
made available. As a result of this bounty, Travellers in other
parts of the country soon flocked to Dublin. Many came with
totally unrealistic expectations: Dublin social workers were often
greeted with requests by migrants for a new wagon or trailer. On
visits to Travellers in rural areas, I was often asked about the great
quantity of goods and trailers the Dublin ISC and other charities
were believed to give away.

As the Settlement Movement spread nationwide with seventy
local committees organized around the country, many of the benefits first available in Dublin soon spread to other areas, although
never on the same scale.[7] The urgency of the Travellers' situation, which the first ISC so effectively communicated to settled
Irish, could not be duplicated outside Dublin.

Urban Settlement Pattern: Tinkers in Dublin

Although much of the following discussion pertains to Travellers in other Irish cities, such as Galway, Cork, and Limerick, the
focus is strictly on Dublin, since it is the Tinkers' adaptation there
that is the subject of following chapters.[8]

---

[7] The seventy local committees which make up the Itinerant Settlement
Movement were organized and are still run by private individuals. They
typically plan and petition for the construction of camping sites, pressure
local authorities to allocate houses to Travellers, offer literacy and cooking classes for adults, and operate a special bus service to transport children
from camps to school. Recently, however, local governments have begun
to take over many of these functions.

[8] Only five municipalities in Ireland are considered cities: Dublin (650,
153); Cork (125,283); Limerick (58,082); Waterford (29,842); and Galway
City (26,295) [S.A. 1971:22].

Plate 4. Travellers camped along a quiet side road on the outskirts of a provincial town, Ennis, Co. Clare. *(Photo by author)*

    Tinker migrants to Dublin tend to settle on the side of the city from which they first enter. Families from northern and northeastern counties camp on the north side of the city, and those from southern counties on the south side. The Liffey River, which flows through the city center and divides Dublin in two equal halves, is the recognized boundary. With time, as the migrants become better acquainted with the city and the Traveller population there, this boundary becomes less important.

    The vast majority of camping locations are on the periphery of the city in the band where suburban housing developments meet agricultural land. Most camps are located in or adjacent to working-class or lower-middle-class public housing. Favored camping locations are those which are within a short walking distance of shops, which have an available source of water, and which are removed from heavy traffic which would endanger the children.

    Tinker encampments in Dublin can be categorized into four basic types (see Table 2). First are the roadside camps in which a number of wagons, tents, and trailers are strung single file along the grassy margin or shoulder of a road. These camps tend to be

Table 2. Location of Tinker Encampments in Dublin

Location	Number of Sites	Number of Families	Average Number of Families per Site
Roadside sites	13	44	3.4
Empty lots and fields	18	115	6.4
Private property with permission	6	6	1.0
Local authority sites	8	122	15
Total	45	287*	6.4

*Approximately sixty families were unaccounted for. Excludes forty Tinker families who were housed.

Source: Author's survey, May 1975.

small, limited by the amount of open space. There are a number of favorite locations which are occupied continuously: when one family or group moves out, others soon move in. In recent years many roadside camps have been eliminated by the local authorities, who have erected such barriers as concrete posts, mounds of earth, and chain-link fences to prevent families from pulling in their trailers and wagons.

Second are empty lots and fields, where the largest number of families are living. In a number of instances the fields are owned by the City Corporation and are scheduled for future development as housing estates and shopping centers. In the interim, the Corporation and local ISCs have encouraged Tinkers to camp in these fields, often to keep them out of areas where local residents would object. Because of the shortage of good camping sites and the increasing flow of migrants into the city, these camps are often large, containing up to thirty families or up to ten times larger than the former rural camps.

Living conditions in both these types of camps are poor, primarily due to the lack of amenities. Electricity, running water, refuse collection, and toilets are all absent. Water must be obtained from nearby houses, shops, or gasoline stations and carried to the camp in buckets or milk churns. The absence of litter bins and regular refuse collection results in an accumulation of

Plate 5. Tinker girls preparing dinner in a roadside camp. Note the hand-made tin mugs. *(Photo by Pat Langan)*

garbage and unwanted scrap and rags, giving the camps a squalid appearance and creating an eyesore for nearby residents. The situation also attracts rats. The lack of toilets means that bushes and hedgerows must be used for this purpose, adding to the squalor. At present the Tinkers' only means of coping with this problem is to shift periodically to new camps or to new locations within the existing camp.

Plate 6. Tinkers camped on a green in a public housing estate in Finglas, Dublin. *(Photo by author)*

Conditions are worse in wet weather when the constant activity around the trailers and wagons churns the soft ground into a sea of mud. It then becomes nearly impossible to keep the interior of the shelters clean.

Plate 7. Father and son in front of their home in Dublin. The shack is constructed of cardboard, plywood, and corrugated iron collected at the city dump. *(Photo by author)*

The third category of campsites consists of those on private property where the owners have given their permission. There are six such sites in Dublin, each for a single family: three are located on convent grounds and three in the backyards of private citizens. Families often do not remain long in these sites, because they soon feel isolated and lonely when on their own.

Official local authority sites constructed specifically for Tinkers are the fourth type of camping location. In 1975 there were eight sites: four small ones built by the Dublin County Council, each with accommodation for four families, and four large sites built by the City Corporation, accommodating an average of twenty-eight families.[9] In all but two cases accommodation is provided in huts which range in size from a single room (known as a *tigin,* Irish for "small house") on the older sites to a five-room shelter or "chalet" on the newer sites. Amenities included electricity, hot and cold running water, toilets, a place to store scrap metal, and, on several sites, communal land for grazing horses.

The first site, Labre Park, was built in 1967 in an industrial area. The land had been a city dump and is crossed by high-tension wires. Nearby factories form a buffer zone between the site and the working-class neighborhood of Ballyfermot. This location was finally accepted after plans to build in several other locations encountered stiff opposition from local residents. The five-acre site houses thirty-seven families in *tigins*, arranged in a single long row with barely 15 feet separating one from the next

---

[9]The Dublin County Council, a body of elected officials, and the civil servants of the Dublin Corporation disagree on the proper size for Tinker sites. The County Council is opposed to large sites on the grounds that they are a nuisance to local residents and that they lead to ghetto-like conditions which retard the integration of the Travellers into settled society. Also, as elected officials, County Councillors are influenced by the prejudices of their constituents, who are opposed to any settlement of itinerants in their neighborhood, but especially on large sites. The City Corporation, on the other hand, is opposed to small sites as being economically unfeasible. It is far less expensive to build and maintain a few large sites where community services can be concentrated than a greater number of small sites.

Plate 8.   Labre Park, the largest and oldest local authority site in Dublin. It accommodates thirty-nine families in small, almost windowless, huts called *Tigins. (Photo by author)*

(see Plate 8). The huts, which measure only 10 feet by 15 feet, were originally designed to be annexes to the Travellers' own trailers or wagons. In fact, ownership of a wagon or trailer was a requirement of tenancy, but many families soon sold their caravans and moved into the small huts. The site offers some grazing land, a primary school exclusively for Traveller children, and a small recreation center. A city employee is on duty round-the-clock to maintain order and to keep the site tidy.

Most Settlement Committee members and local officials hoped that sites such as Labre Park would serve as a sort of half-way house, a place in which families would become accustomed to settled life (or as some saw it, become rehabilitated). Families would then move on to conventional housing in the settled community. However, few families have yet expressed an interest in regular housing; in the eight years since Labre Park opened, only three families have "graduated." Many Travellers, perhaps one-third, now consider the site their permanent home and have no desire to move. Although some families leave each summer to travel, they pay their rent in advance to insure that they will have their *tigin* when they return. The same pattern has been repeated in many other sites around the country.[10]   On a serviced site, many of the advantages of housing are present—running water, toilets, electricity, and access to schools—thus there is little incentive to move away from fellow Travellers into an unfamiliar and sometimes hostile settled community. In recognition that serviced sites do become permanent homes for many families, all local authority sites now under construction must have three bedrooms and full amenities in order to qualify for government subsidies.

In 1975, six additional sites for up to thirty families each were in the planning stage. But local officials fear that even with the new campsites completed they will not be able to keep pace with the expanding population of Tinkers in the city.

Complaints by Neighboring Settled Irish. Campsites and the Travellers themselves are often a nuisance to nearby settled Irish. Despite the sympathy some feel toward itinerants, residents frequently complain about the litter and squalid appearance of the camps, about women and children begging daily at their doors, and occasionally about drunkenness and rowdyism. The most frequent objection among residents near large camps, however, and a cause of great antagonism towards Tinkers, is their wandering horses. The horses which may number up to twenty in one camp, must be let loose to graze. This poses a serious traffic problem. In one incident, a woman was killed when her car collided with a horse on the road at night. The animals may also endanger small children who approach them carelessly. They sometimes damage lawns and gardens in residential areas. At Holylands, the problem was so serious that the local residents' association convened on several occasions to consider the issue. At the one meeting I was asked to attend, residents suggested

---

[10] Outside the Dublin area, there are twenty-four sites which provide *tigins* or chalets and full amenities. There are approximately thirty other campsites which do not have permanent structures: most have a water tap and an asphalt area on which families can park their wagons and trailers; on some, trailers are provided by the local authority or the ISC. In 1975, 368 families or almost 30 percent of the itinerant population (excluding families housed in the settled community in Ireland) were living on official campsites.

that the city officials force the families to give up their animals, and to send them back to the countryside if they refused. On the average, forty-five horses from Holylands were impounded each month.[11]

Prior to the Settlement Movement, there was considerable official opposition to Tinkers camping in the city. At the direction of local authorities, the police regularly evicted them from most campsites. Through the efforts of the Dublin ISC, the manner in which local authorities treat Travellers has improved considerably in recent years. Today police do not generally evict them unless they are creating serious problems for local residents.

---

[11] The owners were charged ninety pence per horse per day in pound fees, and they often received a court summons which led to additional fines. In one instance at Holylands, a man had five horses impounded on four consecutive days, costing him eighteen pounds in fees before he even appeared in court.

CHAPTER FOUR

The Urban
Economic Adaptation

The aim of this chapter is to examine the economic adaptation Tinkers have made in the city, specifically their major subsistence activities and the strategies they use in each. The reasons Travellers have not adopted the employment patterns of settled society are also discussed. Last, family income and consumption patterns are treated.

Scavenging

Scavenging clearly has its roots in the past. While on their traditional rounds peddling goods, sweeping chimneys, and repairing tinware, Tinkers also asked householders for unwanted rags, glass jars, feathers, horsehair, and scrap metal items. Several factors—the obsolescence of their former trades, an increase in scrap metal prices during and after World War II, and the Travellers' migration to urban areas—have made scavenging for scrap metal the major occupation of Tinker men.

Urban Tinkers actually collect anything they can use themselves or sell to someone else. By going door-to-door in residential areas they obtain old mattresses, furniture, deposit bottles, clothing, rags, and—most important—metal items such as worn-out pots and pans, appliances, bicycles, and car batteries. At small local "tips" (garbage dumps) they gather many of these same articles, as well as wood for their fires and for the construction of winter shelters. From businesses, factories, and construction sites they collect obsolete machinery, wire, pipes, and other industrial waste products with metal content.

The following description, based on field notes, typifies the scavenging pattern of most Dublin Travellers.

At eleven o'clock Mick (age 30), his brother Franci (age 21), and their nephew Mylee (age 13) left Holylands on their horse-drawn cart. They rode several miles, passing areas which they had already covered earlier in the week, and finally turned off the main road into a middle-class housing estate. Mick pulled the cart onto the curb where the horse was able to graze on the lawn. The men each took a side of the street while Mylee tended the horse and cart. "Have you any old scrap, mattresses, old batteries, bikes?" Mick asked the woman at the first door. Brusquely, she replied, "No." "Any old clothes or furniture you want to get rid of?" he added quickly before she closed the door. At the end of the block neither man had gotten anything. After learning from one resident that other itinerants had already been through the neighborhood, they decided to drive on to a "fresh" area. At about the tenth house, Mick received the first scrap of the day: an old four-cylinder engine and a set of bald tires. After loading the scrap onto the cart, they returned to the garage for some trash the householder wanted taken away. The man was pleasant, but he watched them closely, undoubtedly to make certain they did not steal anything from his garage.

By one o'clock, after knocking on about fifty doors in this neighborhood, they had collected two small bundles of clothing, a fireplace grate, a rusty bike frame, a broken hair dryer, and the engine and tires. With this amount of scrap, they turned the corner and started working their way out of town back toward Holylands. When passing people in their yards or driveways they called out, "Have you any old scrap . . . batteries . . . old furniture for sale?" Most people ignored them; many did not even look up to acknowledge their presence. Others watched indifferently as the pony and cart trotted by. Only a few actually bothered to shake their head or wave their hands in rejection. Children showed the most interest, and then mainly in the horse and cart. A few ran behind the cart and tried to jump on the back despite the men's protests.

The next stop was at a service station where Travellers are able to get old automobile parts, worn-out tires, and the like. The station manager offered to sell them several expired car batteries at six shillings each. After some bargaining they bought them all for two-thirds the asking price. They canvassed one more neighborhood but received only a stack of *Arizona Highways*—from which Mick later used the pictures to decorate his hut. By three o'clock they returned to camp, their work done for the day. The estimated value of the scrap they collected was two pounds.

Not all scavenging is done from a horse and cart. During
the last fifteen years many Tinkers have acquired vans and lorries
(trucks). Motorized collectors have several advantages over those
with a horse and cart, all of which increase their profits: they
can travel faster, cover a wider territory, and transport heavier
loads. For these reasons some have become middlemen, purchasing scrap metal from horse-and-cart collectors who are unable to
transport their steel and iron to the central city metal merchants
or foundries. A few travel to small towns outside Dublin to
purchase scrap from Travellers there, often for half the price it
brings from the city metal merchants.

Some motorized collectors solicit solely from businesses and
factories. This requires a sizeable amount of capital, since large
items such as machinery are purchased. Although this involves
certain risks—for example, a dealer must be able to judge accurately
the weight of the metal he will have after all nonmetallic parts
have been stripped away—the profits are larger than in scavenging
from householders. Jim and Dan Brien, for example, bought five
aluminum diesel engines and a large reel of used electric wire from
a factory for one hundred pounds. After three days of work breaking the engines down into piles of aluminum, steel, and copper
(from the generators) and burning the rubber insulation from the
wire, they realized a profit of eighty pounds. Several months
passed, however, before they were able to make another such remunerative deal.

In recent years many shopowners, householders, and tradesmen have become aware of the value of scrap, especially of nonferrous metals such as copper, lead, aluminum, and brass; many
are no longer willing to give scrap items away free. Thus manipulative strategies have increased in importance. Many of the
tactics Travellers use in dealing are not unlike those used in past
economic transactions with settled Irish.

In an attempt to overcome the antagonism many house-
dwellers feel toward itinerants and their hesitancy to interact with
them, scrap dealers are forced to be aggressive and persistent.
When first approaching a person for scrap, they quickly request a
long list of items in hopes of triggering a response. "Have you
any old scrap . . . mattresses . . . batteries . . . old furniture for
sale?" A good dealer then dominates the conversation, keeping

up a steady flow of forceful yet friendly conversation in order to
ward off a refusal, eventually convincing the householder to do
business with him. Some may attempt to play upon the householder's sympathies by inventing hardship stories. It is not uncommon for men to swear on their own or their children's lives—
"that I may fall down paralyzed dead if I'm telling you a lie"—
to prove their sincerity. Verbal skills similar to those required
of a salesman are essential to being a successful dealer.

Men often work together in persuading a householder or
shopowner to do business with them, especially when a large
transaction is involved. With a mixture of hesitancy and enthusiasm, they seek to create the illusion that the settled person is
getting an excellent bargain, and that they are being drawn to
an agreement only with great reluctance. They may feign dis-
interest in items which would actually be of value to them, bargaining enthusiastically for a relatively worthless object; only
later to return, seemingly with reluctance, to the desired goods.
As in the past, they often give advice and instructions, such as
the value of the object or the price to bid, to each other in
Gammon. Commands are spoken rapidly and just enough *Gammon*
vocabulary is used to camouflage what is being said. Because of
this the settled person who overhears a conversation may not
realize that the Tinkers are attempting to communicate secretly;
instead he assumes that they are speaking garbled English and
that he has misunderstood a word or two. The fact that most
settled folk are not even aware that Travellers possess their own
argot is testimony to its success.

Apart from the economic necessity involved, Travellers view
dealing with settled Irish as a personal challenge—a battle of wits
and a test of their cleverness. Most feel little or no guilt at
exploiting settled Irish when the opportunity arises; they believe
it is up to each individual, itinerant and settled alike, to protect
his own interests. As Braroe (1965) has pointed out with respect
to Canadian Prairie Indians who occasionally swindle local whites,
such practices raise the self-image of the outcast group and thereby help to avoid destructive loss of identity. The following example,
though not common, illustrates some of the above points. Accompanied by his brother-in-law, Marty asked for scrap at the home of
a retired police officer. Earlier, while out begging, Marty's wife

noticed scrap in the man's yard. The policeman led them to a shed where two automobile engines, several batteries, and a large pile of old aluminum siding were stored. As in most transactions, rather than make an offer which might be higher than the settled person would have asked, Marty insisted that the policeman state his price first. When he asked eight pounds for each of the two engines, Marty realized that the man did not know the value of his scrap metal, because the aluminum siding was worth several times more than the engines. With this in mind, Marty bargained enthusiastically for the engines, reluctantly agreeing in the end to pay fourteen pounds if the other "old stuff" was thrown in as well. The policeman agreed, and the Travellers quickly loaded the aluminum siding and batteries onto their lorry, promising to return later for the engines. That afternoon they sold the aluminum and the battery lead alone for twenty pounds. They never returned to pick up the engines, much less to pay the owner the promised amount.

The settled person who is swindled has little recourse, since few incidents are serious enough to warrant police action. In addition, the police often have difficulty bringing Tinkers to justice, for they can escape court summons simply by shifting to a new camp or adopting a different name.

Plate 9.   Unloading from a cart items collected scavenging, Holylands camp, Dublin. The boy in background is placing the articles in different piles according to type. *(Photo by Pat Langan)*

The first task for all scavengers upon returning to camp is to separate the scrap they have collected according to type. Objects made of nonferrous metals must then be "cleaned:" all foreign material, such as the plastic handles on pots and pans, must be removed before the metal can be sold to a metal merchant. The laborious task of removing the nonmetallic parts is usually performed by young boys equipped only with a hammer and chisel. Sometimes fire is used, as in removing insulation from copper wire. Frequently the fires are fueled with rubber tires which give off noxious clouds of black smoke, creating a nuisance for nearby residents as well as other families in camp. Once cleaned, the more valuable nonferrous metals are placed in sacks and hidden inside or beneath the wagons and trailers until they are taken to the metal merchant. The bits of plastic, rubber, paper, and other leftover materials, as well as items collected which cannot be sold, litter the camps and give them a squalid appearance.

The bulkier and less valuable steel and iron is left outside. When a pile of several tons has accumulated, it is transported to the large scrap yard of Hammond-Lane Company on the Dublin waterfront. There Tinkers drive their loaded trucks or carts onto scales to be weighed, proceed to the scrap yard and remove the load by hand, and then return to the scales to have the empty lorry weighed and to receive payment.[1]

Travellers sometimes attempt to maximize their profit by concealing "dirt," or foreign material, in with their scrap in order to increase its weight. Some filled copper radiators with sand until metal merchants learned of the practice and began checking. After that, some men would occasionally pour molten lead into the radiators; this could not easily be detected without sawing the radiator in half. Copper tubing is often filled with mud, and pieces of iron are sometimes placed in the burlap bags along with valuable nonferrous metals to add weight. In most transactions, so much metal is being handled that merchants do not have the time to check each load thoroughly. If "dirt" is found, however, or if the metal has not been properly cleaned, the Tinker is forced

---

[1] In July 1975, prices per ton of metal were: iron, £25; steel, £14. Prices per one hundred pounds (.05 ton) of nonferrous metals were: copper, £19; brass, £13.50; lead £5; and aluminum, £5 to £8, depending on quality.

Plate 10.   Two Travellers unloading their scrap at a metal merchant's
yard in central Dublin.   *(Photo by author)*

either to accept a reduced rate or to take the load away. Because
Travellers form an important part of the metal merchants' clientele,
however, they are rarely told not to return.

Sometimes Travellers themselves are swindled in transactions
with metal merchants, most often because of their illiteracy. Because they are unable to read the scales or the receipts they are
given, they may easily be cheated. James Gavin, who is semiliterate
after spending six years in an industrial school (reformatory) as a
youth, sold a load of iron and steel worth forty pounds on the
scales but was paid only thirty pounds in cash. He did not realize
the discrepancy until he was sitting in a pub several hours later
and happened to look at his receipt, something most men immediately discard.

Other items obtained by scavenging are sold to specialized merchants. About once a month a dealer in second-hand mattresses visits the various Dublin camps. He pays up to fifty pence for each mattress the men have collected. Torn or otherwise unsaleable clothing was sold to rag merchants until recently. Now the prices given for rags are so low that most Tinkers no longer consider this practice worthwhile. Furniture, appliances, bikes, and especially second-hand clothing are sold each Saturday morning in an outdoor market in central Dublin known as "the Hill." Most of the money earned at the market comes from the sale of used clothing to the Dublin poor.

The Travellers' scavenging serves a valuable economic and ecological function in Irish society. Tons of steel, iron, copper, lead, and other metals would be wasted if not reclaimed in this way; the Travellers also recycle used clothing, appliances, and furniture from the middle class to the poor. Dublin metal merchants estimate that Tinkers account for about half of all the scrap metal collected outside of industry. Significantly, they gather the odd bits and pieces—the broken toasters, worn-out washing machines, and rusted drain pipes—that large-scale settled dealers do not bother with. Travellers also save the city of Dublin considerable expense each year by clearing away the hundreds of abandoned or dumped autos.

In relation to the hours spent, the return from scavenging is small. About 75 to 80 percent of the metal Tinkers gather is the less valuable iron and steel. Furthermore, the supply of the valuable nonferrous metals is declining because such items as drain pipes and water pipes, once made of lead or copper, are now made of plastic. In the last few years earnings from scavenging have also decreased as a result of competition from other Travellers moving into the city and from some unemployed settled Irish who have taken up this activity. And, as previously mentioned, householders and businessmen who once gave scrap away free now ask Tinkers to pay for it.

While scavenging, Tinkers are alert to other economic opportunities. At the doors they often ask about odd jobs such as cleaning up a yard and hauling trash to the dump. Upon noticing a driveway in need of repair, they may persuade the owner to have it resurfaced and do the work themselves or sell the job to friends who have the proper equipment. They often deal in second-hand items. People in need of an automobile or bicycle part or some other gadget frequently ask Tinkers, knowing there is a good chance they may have it in their scrap piles.

The following example illustrates one scavenger's ingenuity. Red Mick knocked on the door of one house and made the usual request for scrap, listing a variety of items the woman might have. When she replied that she had none and was in fact looking for a used bike, Mick immediately asked for details about the type of bike she wanted. Three weeks later, another householder showed Mick some articles in his garage that he wished to sell, including a bicycle. Mick bargained for and purchased the bike; then, although he could not read street names or even house numbers, he returned to the woman's house and sold it to her at a profit of five pounds.

Tinkers also adjust to the seasonal demands of suburban homeowners in the same way their traditional trades and services followed the seasonal cycle of farmwork. During the spring, when householders begin to trim their hedges and lawns, for example, many seek jobs sharpening lawn mowers and hedge clippers. Since this is also the time for "spring cleaning," Travellers also get jobs cleaning yards and hauling trash to the dump. At Christmas, some men cut holly and conifers for Christmas trees in neighboring rural areas and sell them in bulk to shop-keepers or door-to-door in the suburbs. In a similar fashion, some children sell clusters of freshly cut shamrocks on St. Patrick's Day.

The recent boom in "roadside trading" involving several hundred families provides another example of the Travellers' flexibility and opportunism. This activity involves selling new consumer goods such as radios, portable televisions, blankets, and umbrellas from tables set up on the roadside. It emerged suddenly after a few families discovered that large quantities of merchandise from smoke damaged and bombed-out stores in Northern Ireland were available at low prices. The first traders smuggled these goods across isolated border roads without paying duty and began selling them along the main roads in the Republic. As settled folk looking for bargains and enjoying the haggling over prices bought furiously, other Tinkers took up the trade. Some bought goods in small lots and imported them legally into the Republic under a new law which allows each individual to bring in goods valued up to fifty-two pounds duty free. Trading became so brisk that local businessmen complained. A spokesman for the Radio and Television Manufacturers' Association claimed that the industry had lost half a million pounds in one year because of the Tinkers' roadside selling and threatened that unless it was stopped hundreds of workers would be laid off. Despite raids by police and customs officials, many families continue to trade. Now that they have satisfied much of the demand for cheap radios and the like, many have switched to new wares such as carpets which they roll out along the grassy shoulder of the road.

Begging

Traditionally, begging was an adjunct to peddling. As Traveller women bartered or sold small household wares such as needles, lace, and brushes, they also solicited alms. With the decline in the importance of rural peddling, women turned exclusively to begging. Today, begging both on the city streets and from door to door in the suburbs is the primary occupation of Traveller women in the city and a major source of income in most families

"House begging"—the door-to-door solicitation of alms—is more common than "street begging," perhaps because it is more closely related to the former peddling-begging routine Travellers are familiar with. There is also less stigma attached to it than to street begging, which has become common only in recent years. Every day of the week except Sunday, women walk from house to house in Dublin's suburbs asking for alms.

As in scavenging, there are few rules governing the selection of a neighborhood in which to beg and there are no exclusive begging territories. Neighborhoods are selected more or less at random, although if a woman learns that another Traveller has "worked" the same houses within the past few days, she will move on to a new neighborhood. Most avoid returning to the same neighborhood until one or two weeks have passed.

The begging strategies of Traveller women in Dublin appear to have changed little from those used in former times. The beggar's basic objective is to evoke sympathy and compassion in the housewife so she will give alms. This is accomplished by what

Goffman (1959) has called "impression management": Tinkers work to create the impression that they are destitute and sincerely in need of help. To this end a number of ploys are used. The most obvious is the manipulation of dress and general appearance. Although a woman may own one or two "respectable" outfits, she wears old clothing, often soiled and tattered, when begging. She may also wear the traditional shawl or "rug," an unmistakable symbol of the beggar's identity as a Tinker as well as a reminder of the past poverty of rural Ireland, when all peasant women wore the shawl. The importance of presenting the right image is demonstrated by the lack of success some—particularly unmarried, teenage girls—experience when they fail to dress appropriately. Sensitive about their appearance in public and less concerned about maximizing profits, since most give the earnings to their parents, some teenagers wear short skirts, neat blouses or sweaters, and even makeup. The amount of alms they receive is only a fraction of what other women get.

The demeanor the beggar assumes at the door is also important. Most women feign great humility. Their eyes are held downcast and their plea for alms is stated softly, in an urgent voice bordering on a whine. Their humility, however, may quickly change to hostility or abuse if they are turned away rudely or abruptly.

All Travellers' pleas for alms share several characteristics. They retain the traditional practice of asking for small amounts, such as "a bit of help," "a bit of change," or "a sup of milk" to make a refusal seem especially miserly. They also appeal to the religious values of Irish society by making frequent references to God or to Christianity. A typical plea for alms might begin with the phrase "God Bless you ma'am" and include additional references to God throughout. Beggars often conclude requests with the promise to say a prayer for the person. The intent of such references is not only to remind the house-dweller of her Christian obligation to help the less fortunate, but also to give the impression that the beggar herself is religious. This strategy was particularly successful in the past, according to one Irishman:

> It was held to be an unlucky thing to turn a travelling person away, especially if they asked for help in the name of God (I.F.C. 1952b [vol. 1218] :192).

Invariably the beggar uses the plural "us" rather than the singular "me." In this way Travellers attempt to show that their main concern is for their children rather than themselves. Thus a typical begging plea might begin as follows:

> God bless you, ma'am. Could you give us a bit of help? Maybe you'd have a bit of change so I could buy me childer a bottle of milk.

And if the housewife refuses or hesitates, the beggar might add:

> Holy Mary, Mother of God, I don't care about meself, ma'am, it's the poor childer I'm afeard for. They've nothin' to eat this two days.

In an attempt to convince the housewife that their poverty stems from circumstances beyond their control rather than from squandering money, beggars may provide additional details or even fabricate hardship stories. References to illness are common: "Me poor man is sick this three weeks with a bad chest." Some women, aware that many Dubliners stereotype Tinker men as lazy, irresponsible drunkards, appeal directly to these prejudices by claiming that their husbands have deserted them.

The presence of a child or infant is an important element of begging strategy. As a rule, a small child accompanies the beggar on foot or a baby is pushed along in a pram. Travellers are acutely aware that much of the concern settled Irish express toward them is actually sympathy for their children. If the beggar does not have a small child of her own, she may borrow one from another family in camp. One three-year-old at Holy-lands, whose cute face and amusing antics proved to be a considerable asset in begging, was borrowed regularly by other women.

When the above strategies fail, Tinkers often rely on persistence to wear the settled person down. They realize that many housewives can be made to give alms by creating a nuisance—refusing to leave the door and repeating their requests over and over.

Although Travellers prefer to receive money, they are usually given food and used clothing. Many people are reluctant to give cash because they believe it will be spent on drink by Traveller men. The beggar places the alms she receives in a pram or shopping bag she carries with her. As the bag or pram fills up, the goods are sorted; unwanted items are sometimes tossed out on the spot. These include clothing which cannot be used or sold and prepared or opened food which might be stale or contaminated. Understandably, householders who find the goods thrown in their yards tend to become angry.

Not all begging requires the active manipulation of settled people. After numerous visits to the same houses, Travellers sometimes become acquainted with housewives on a personal basis, and a type of patroness-client relationship develops. In such cases housewives give exclusively to one or two Tinkers, turning others away. Traveller women may have a number of patronesses whom they refer to as their "ladies." On the average they visit their ladies once every two or three weeks, in some cases on a prearranged day. In patroness-client relationships the amount of alms given is greater than that obtained through random begging, and the amount and type of goods often becomes standardized. Katie Brien, for example, regularly received two tins of vegetables, two pounds of sugar, one-half pound of tea, one jar of jam, and four shillings in cash from one patroness; occasionally she received used clothing as well.

In the more established patroness-client relationships social barriers are partially broken down, and the Traveller is often invited into the home of her lady for tea and biscuits. Occasionally she assists with light housework such as dusting and drying dishes. In conversation, the Traveller may relate her family problems and the latest gossip about other families in camp. The patroness, in turn, may give friendly although often paternalistic advice about hygiene, cooking, and other domestic activities. Travellers often rely on their ladies for assistance in writing letters and in dealing with police, court, and welfare officials. Two patronesses of one Holylands woman posted bail for her husband's release from jail. Another patroness, whose husband was a high-ranking civil servant, pressured Dublin housing authorities into allocating a house to her client's family.

Upon returning to camp at the end of the day, women sort through the goods they have received. Much of the food—which consists mainly of bread, sugar, tinned vegetables, soup, and tea— is consumed that evening and the following morning. Clothing is

Plate 11.   Traveller woman selling second-hand clothing on "The Hill" in central Dublin. *(Photo by Pat Langan)*

sorted into two piles: one for home use and a second for sale on "the Hill." It is impossible to place a precise monetary value on the items Tinkers receive, but the cost of purchasing such food and clothing would be substantial. Begging provides most women with enough clothing to outfit the entire family (even if they have to swap with other women to get the right sizes) and the food they receive often comprises one-fourth or more of their daily consumption. Although the amount of cash received is small, rarely more than five or six shillings, the weekly cash income derived from selling surplus clothing may amount to five pounds or more.

Plate 12. Traveller girl and child begging on O'Connell Bridge in Dublin.
(Photo by Pat Langan)

Street begging takes place in the busy shopping and business districts of downtown Dublin where pedestrian traffic is heavy. Most beggars walk up and down the street with outstretched hand, soliciting money from passers-by. A few sit on the sidewalk, usually near the entrance to large department stores, with a small cardboard box at their side.

Street begging is most profitable on Friday, payday for most settled Irish, and Saturday, the major shopping day. On these days beggars earn about one pound more than usual. On holidays, particularly Christmas, their earnings are often doubled. Otherwise, begging is best during good weather, when pedestrians and shoppers are in less of a hurry to get inside and off the street.

The verbal strategies used in street begging are basically the same as those employed in the suburbs. But because the encounter between Tinker and pedestrian is so brief, the visual impression created by the beggar becomes more important than her verbal plea. Here the presence of an infant or small child is considered crucial. Even adolescent girls too young to be mothers take along an infant which they present as their own. Alternatively, women may stuff their shawls with clothing or rags to give the appearance of a baby. They sometimes do this simply to avoid the burden of carrying an infant back and forth along the street all day. This is not possible in house begging, where encounters are longer and the housewife may ask to see the child.

As in other dealings with settled people, persistence is the strategy of last resort. By pursuing an individual along the sidewalk, the beggar is often able to manipulate the person into giving. Some will follow a likely prospect as much as twenty yards up the street. By her continued presence and occasionally by her boisterous talk, the Traveller makes it apparent to other pedestrians on the street that this particular individual is refusing to give alms. Wishing to avoid a further scene, the person may give simply to escape the beggar and the undesired attention.

Street begging is generally more profitable than house begging, since only cash is received. In the three to four hours women spend begging each day they earn an average of three pounds. The usual gratuity is small, however, ranging from five to ten pence. The occasional fifty pence piece or pound note is something to boast about back in camp.

To many women, the major drawback to street begging is its illegality. It carries a maximum penalty of one month imprisonment. Enforcement of the anti-begging statutes, however, is sporadic. The women who beg on city streets are frequently warned and chased off, but they are rarely arrested. The summer tourist season—when city officials are most sensitive about Dublin's public image—is the only time street beggars are seriously bothered by the police.

Some of the begging strategies employed by Tinkers, both on the streets and in the neighborhoods, have negative consequences which ultimately detract from the amount of sympathy and alms they receive. Street beggars who become aggressive or threatening may receive immediate alms, but the hostility they create lessens the likelihood that the individual will give more alms in the future. The house beggars' practice of discarding unwanted clothing and food in the front gardens of the people who have given to them also works to their disadvantage. After one or two such incidents, house-dwellers often cease giving to Travellers. In my discussions with settled people this was a frequent complaint.

Since begging strategies are designed to evoke sympathy and compassion, how can such contradictory behavior be explained? Like Gypsies and most other nomadic groups, Tinkers have always focused on short-term subsistence activities—which sometimes included pilfering from gardens and hen houses—while ignoring the long-range effects their predatory behavior might have on their relationship with the host society. Because of their mobility, they were usually able to avoid the consequences of their behavior. The begging practice of urban Tinkers follows the same pattern: most concentrate on getting the most out of the exchange taking place at the moment. This is not true in every case, however, and some women are highly critical of those who give Tinkers a bad name.

For some Tinkers, openly dropping clothing and food in the front gardens of those who gave is a gesture of the contempt many Travellers feel toward settled society and its neglect and mistreatment of itinerants. It demonstrates that the alms given are not enough to repay Travellers for the hardships and discrimination they have endured and that they will not accept just any charity. One beggar remarked, "They think just because you ask for something, that you'll take anything and be happy with it."

Welfare

Welfare benefits make up an important part of the average
family's income. It was not until the 1950s, when Tinkers first
migrated to urban areas, that they began receiving benefits even
on a small scale. Today nearly all families receive Unemployment
Assistance and the Children's Allowance; many get other benefits,
such as Home Assistance, Deserted Wife's Allowance, and old age
pensions. In 1975 a married man with two dependent children
under age 16 received £12.55 weekly from the dole and £5.00
each month in Children's Allowance. For each additional child,
the dole increased by £1.25 and the Children's Allowance by £3.75.

A few Tinkers, such as large-scale scrap dealers who have incomes which might disqualify them from receiving the dole, sign
up at labor exchanges in the neighboring towns of Dun Laoghaire
and Bray. In this way they avoid detection by welfare inspectors
who make spot checks on the families in their jurisdiction to determine their eligibility. Because many Tinkers are not permanently
settled and change camps frequently, it is difficult to prove that a
family is not living in the district of its labor exchange.

In addition to State welfare payments, a number of private
charity organizations such as the Society of St. Vincent de Paul
and the Irish Sisters of Charity offer assistance to needy families.
Travellers utilize these resources whenever the need or opportunity
arises. While out scavenging, for example, men occasionally ask for
a meal at a convent, and at Christmas some families turn to them
for toys for their children. Travellers are also able to obtain travel
expenses in certain instances, usually in order to be reunited with
their children or spouse. The case of Biddy Cassidy is not unusual.
After a severe "row" with her husband in which she received a
black eye and a cut lip, she took four of her ten children and left
their caravan home in Manchester to return to Ireland. Several
weeks later she received word from England that her husband was
threatening to place the remaining six children in a foster home
unless she returned. Biddy immediately conveyed this news to
the nuns at a nearby convent; she was given money for a round-
trip ticket to England to retrieve her children and return to Ireland.

Travellers' attitudes towards receiving welfare vary, but in
general they feel little stigma. The fact that many settled folk

also receive the dole and that people of all income levels are eligible for Children's Allowance reduces the shame that Tinkers, the outcasts, might otherwise feel. Nevertheless, some middle-aged and older Tinkers are not completely happy receiving "hand-outs," even though these cash benefits have raised their standard of living and made life easier. The Travellers themselves frequently voice the complaint that many have become so reliant on welfare that they have lost their pride and are unwilling to care for themselves.

> The Travellin' People are goin' pure savage over all these hand-outs. The men don't know what to do with themselves. It has more of them gone pure stupid with drink. Years ago Travellers never had much money to spare for drink, now they're livin' in the pubs. The women only have to get on a bus that takes them into the city and stick out their hand to make their livin'. Travellin' People today have no respect in themselves. Too many people is doin' too much for 'em. If they really want to do good, they'll give the men work and stop payin' em for doin' nothin' (Biddy Connors, age 74).

Members of the younger generation have fewer qualms. They have been raised in an environment in which it is natural for men to draw the dole and women to collect the Children's Allowance and other benefits; they know no other way of life, nor do they recall the past. These families view State welfare and institutional charities as just another social resource to be utilized. Boys look forward to their eighteenth birthday, the day they become eligible to receive Unemployment Assistance. Families, especially husbands, often want more children in order to increase their benefits. This was apparent in a change in attitudes toward family planning which followed a hefty government increase in welfare benefits. At the time of my first research in 1971-72, many young couples ex-pressed a sincere desire to have smaller families and sought in-formation on birth control pills and various contraceptive devices. Three years later, after the dole and Children's Allowance incre-ments for each dependent had increased—by 250 percent in the first case—there was noticeably less interest in having fewer child-ren. One informant calculated to me in raw economic terms why he wanted more children, although he already had eleven.

Unlike welfare, a more or less automatic handout which all families receive, Tinkers view private institutional charity as a resource under the control of social workers who dispense it as they see fit. Thus Traveller women, who in most families handle interaction with outsiders, seek to establish and maintain good relations with social workers. The verbal skills and other tactics of persuasion used to manipulate settled folk when begging are also employed when dealing with charities. One informant wore several religious medals whenever she approached the nearby Sisters of Charity convent for help. Another Holylands family displayed a large picture of Christ in a prominent place on their trailer wall, largely for the effect it would have on visits by a devout social worker.

Wage Labor

In 1975, fewer than twenty-five men and women, less than 4 percent of the adult Tinker population of Dublin, held conventional jobs. Why have so few adopted the employment patterns of settled society? To begin with, the only jobs they are able to obtain are typically low-paying, menial, and monotonous: construction, factory assembly-line, janitorial, and domestic work. And even these jobs are difficult to obtain. All but approximately 5 percent of adult Travellers are illiterate; this automatically excludes them from many jobs. But more important in the case of unskilled work are the prejudices of employers. Many employers have a stereotyped image of Tinkers as both lazy and irresponsible and refuse to consider them. Nearly all my informants had been turned down for work at least once upon being unable to give a street address. "Once you tell 'em you live in a camp, that's it, you're finished, you may as well get up and go out the door." One girl who found work as a waitress was later fired when her employer discovered that she was a Tinker.

Certain subcultural traits also mediate against regular employment. Tinkers value their independence—their freedom to determine for themselves when they will work, for what period of time, and at what task. Most jobs obviously do not allow such choices. The work patterns of settled society involve a great deal of regimentation—regular hours, specific tasks, and, on the assembly line, a fixed pace. Tinkers, like Gypsies (Sutherland 1975; Adams et al.

1975) and many other traditionally self-employed and self-sufficient groups, object to the loss of autonomy required by conventional employment. In fact, much of America's industrial labor force is beginning to develop the same sentiments, which are reflected in increasing job turnover and absenteeism.

For Travellers, employment also means submission to the decisions and commands of settled people and a heightened awareness of their own inferior status with respect to settled society. Among American Gypsies, rejection of regular wage labor in the host society takes the form of a ritual taboo.

> In general, any employment that requires close contact with non-Gypsies or puts a person under the direction and authority of a non-Gypsy is avoided. This kind of employment is considered *marime* (polluted) because it requires some kind of commitment to American society and contradicts important values of Rom society (Sutherland 1975:72).

Tinkers who obtain wage labor are often given the most demeaning tasks. Mickalou, who worked for a month as a custodian at a Dublin plant, was assigned to clean the toilets and washrooms while his co-workers performed less degrading tasks.

Moreover, most jobs simply do not pay enough to overcome other drawbacks. Men can usually earn as much from the dole and scavenging as from regular employment. With six children—an average size family—a man receives almost eighteen pounds a week on the dole, leaving only seven pounds to be earned by scavenging in order to bring his weekly income to that of most unskilled workers. The more children a man has the less the incentive to work since the dole, like other welfare benefits, increases with the number of dependents. Paddy Flynn, with thirteen children, receives £26.30 at the labor exchange each week. A regular job would mean an actual reduction in income. The wages paid to women are especially poor. In 1972, several women from Labre Park obtained cleaning jobs in a nearby plant at ten pounds per week. Within a few months most had quit, explaining that they could make more money begging and would enjoy it more.

In general, regular wage labor is desirable only for young unmarried men, who earn very little (£5.35 per week) on the

dole, and for unmarried women who have no income unless
they beg. Despite the initial enthusiasm of those young adults
who do get jobs, they do not often keep them for long. Over
a period of several months Michael Driscoll, age 21, went to
numerous construction sites and factories in search of work, but
he had no success despite his previous experience in England as
a builder's laborer. Finally through the efforts of a social worker
he obtained a job washing windows for a Dublin cleaning firm.
The work was fairly light, and the wages of twenty-two pounds
per week were more than he had expected. Michael clearly enjoyed his steady income. With his earnings he went to the
movies or pubs almost every evening, purchased his first suit of
new clothes, and bought small gifts for his mother and brothers,
all of which gave him certain prestige. Yet by the third week
he began to lose interest and started arriving at work late. The
following week he quit.

Part of the reason Michael did not remain at work lies in
the factors previously discussed. But other, less obvious reasons
also make it difficult for Michael and others like him to keep a
conventional job. The environment in which most Tinkers live
is one problem. Large camps are noisy until late at night: the
screams and yells of children playing and of family arguments
penetrate the thin walls of wagons and trailers, making it difficult
to sleep until well after midnight. Crowded sleeping conditions
and the presence of a small baby in the same room may add to
the difficulty of getting adequate rest. Awakening on time is
also problematic, as many Tinkers cannot tell time or do not
own clocks. Because of a poor diet—high in starches and low in
protein—many men lack the stamina necessary to work an eight-
hour day, especially in jobs such as construction work which
demand physical labor.

There is also a strong levelling tendency within Traveller
society which can result in the application of negative sanctions
against an individual who takes a job and thus appears to be
rising above his proper station in life. Even men who do not
themselves desire jobs do not like to see others obtain them.
During the three weeks Michael worked for the cleaning firm,
he was the target of much abusive gossip. His peers, envious of
the money he was able to spend on drink and movies, ridiculed

him for having to get up at eight o'clock in the morning and for struggling back to camp exhausted in the evening. Some derisively called him "buffer" and "margarine eater"—pejorative labels Holy-landers used for settled people.

For many Travellers, lack of self-esteem based on the experience and awareness of their pariah status in settled society, leads to the fatalistic expectation that they will fail at a conventional job. The belief of many Traveller men that they are unable to keep a job for more than a short time tends to become a self-fulfilling prophecy. The day after Michael quit his job he commented, "I was lucky to stay on for three weeks. That's pretty good for a Traveller."

A final note: the tendency of Tinkers to quit their jobs after a short period cannot always be interpreted as a failure to cope with the rigors of employment. They often view a job as a means to acquire enough capital to purchase a specific item, such as a caravan, a truck, or even a radio. Once the necessary capital has been obtained, there is no longer any incentive to continue working. Unlike most settled folk, Travellers do not derive other benefits, such as high status or prestige, from being employed.

Family Income and Consumption Patterns

It is difficult to estimate a family's earnings accurately because of the variable nature of scavenging and begging and the difficulty of placing a cash value on the goods collected. Nevertheless, it is clear that most Tinker families in Dublin earn as much—from scavenging, begging, and welfare—as the average blue-collar worker. There are a few families, perhaps 5 percent of the urban Traveller community, who make far more. These are mostly families in which the men are highly successful scrap dealers or oradside traders; a few are families with a large number of children who receive substantial welfare payments and who also beg. At the other end of the scale are the perhaps 10 to 15 percent of Dublin itinerants who live at a bare subsistence level. In many of the poorest families, the adults have a severe drinking problem which prevents them from doing much work.

In one afflicted Holylands family, the diet consisted solely of tea, bread and butter, and an odd assortment of canned foods which the children managed to beg; the cash income from welfare went for drink.

Family incomes also fluctuate seasonally. They are lowest in the winter, when inclement weather often prevents women from begging and men from scavenging. Equally important for many families, the winter—beginning with the Christmas holidays— is a period of heavy drinking and therefore little work. Income is greatest during the spring and summer when begging is lucrative, largely because of tourists, and scavenging is profitable because of homeowners' "spring cleaning."

Tinkers have relatively few expenses in comparison with house-dwellers. With the exception of families on official sites who pay a nominal rent for their huts or chalets, they have no rent or mortgage payments and no gas, electric, water, or other utility bills to pay. And with much of their food and clothing obtained through begging, most of their cash income is free to be spent in other areas. Drink, cigarettes, food, and gas for lorry owners are major family expenses.

As yet, most families spend little money on consumer goods. What possessions Travellers do have are usually acquired second-hand. Clothing, footwear, bedding, and home furnishings—which seldom include more than a few chairs and a table, several pictures or old calendars to decorate the wall, beds (invariably shared by several individuals), and perhaps a bureau—are all obtained through scavenging or begging. As a mobile population, they have traditionally limited their property to what they could carry with them. Among motorized families today this is less of a problem. But other aspects of their lifestyle, notably the lack of electricity, eliminates most home appliances and a wide range of goods.

In recent years, as the standard of living of Travellers has risen, some families have begun to purchase consumer goods such as battery-operated television sets and Primus camp stoves. The wealthiest families have purchased second caravans, called "show trailers," in which they keep a profusion of ornamental knick-knacks and antiques. Most of the family's capital, however, is usually put into a car or van, which among younger men is replacing the horse as the symbol of wealth.

Savings are also becoming more common. Women often place part of the money they earn begging in a postal savings account. Men usually save by investing in horses, and to a lesser extent in carts, trailers, and wagons, which can easily be converted into cash should the need arise. Mares double one's investment almost every year by producing a foal, and they are a source of prestige for their owners. Younger Tinkers who wish to avoid the problems involved in keeping horses in the city may invest their capital in a van or lorry. As they accumulate more capital they trade for newer, more expensive vehicles. When cash is needed, it is easily raised by "swapping down"—trading the vehicle to another Traveller for a less expensive model plus cash. This is similar to the traditional pattern of horse trading in which a man would swap his animal for a horse of lesser quality plus a sum of money known as "the boot."

Another frequent means by which Dublin Travellers raise cash is pawning their valuables—gold rings, radios, accordians, and the like. The usual cost is twenty-five pence per pawn ticket, and they have six months to redeem the item before it becomes the property of the shop. One Holylands family regularly pawned their valuables during the course of each month; then, upon receiving the monthly Children's Allowance, they redeemed them, only to begin pawning again a short while later.

Conclusion

The economic adaptation Tinkers have made in the city is not as different from their former rural adaptation as it may at first appear. Although most Travellers no longer practice their former trades and many have become dependent on welfare for much of their income, the niche they occupy is essentially the same. First, urban Travellers have not become part of the urban proletariat but continue to be self-employed, retaining the freedom to determine their own work schedule and activities. Second, their work is characterized by diversity and flexibility. They continue to practice a variety of activities to satisfy their subsistence needs, and they are quick to take advantage of opportunities. At the doors of settled folk, for example, the urban scavenger not only asks for scrap items but determines if the householder has any other needs he might fill—cleaning up, hauling, resurfacing a driveway, selling second-hand goods. In just the same way the tinsmith was quick to exploit opportunities to repair items other than tinware, to sell or swap a horse, cut turf, thin beet, or perform other farm jobs. Third, the nuclear family continues to be the unit of production and consumption. All members of the family contribute to the family income, including young girls who beg and boys who scavenge and clean scrap. With the exception of men who sometimes team up with a kinsman to scavenge, there is no economic cooperation between families. And finally, because their adaptation involves the utilization of limited resources—alms and scrap items—and the performance of odd jobs for which there is limited demand, mobility is still required. With the tremendous population of urban areas, however, the same degree of travel is not required. And since many Travellers now have motorized transport, they can remain in the same campsite and still travel to a different neighborhood to scavenge or beg each day, rather than moving their camps to each new area in which they work, as they formerly did.

Though the economic niche is basically unaltered, certain changes in the content (as opposed to the structure) of their adaptation have had important consequences for other aspects of Traveller culture. The increased importance of the woman's contribution to family maintenance relative to the man's has affected husband-wife relations, as we will discuss in Chapter Six. There has also been an increase in the level of dependence. Although Tinkers have always relied on charity to some degree, alms and welfare benefits make up a major part of many family's income today.

It is difficult to predict what the long-range effects of the Tinkers' dependence will be. The attitudes of the present generation seem to indicate that dependence on welfare and the gratuities of private citizens and institutions is becoming ingrained. For some, what was first a reaction or adaptation to new resources is becoming a way of life. A look at the fate of groups who have been on public assistance for several generations, including the Appalachian mountaineers and many North American Indians, may indicate some of the consequences of dependence. Caudill describes the effects of welfare on the Kentucky hillbilly forced out of work by automation and the closing of many coal mines:

> The enervating influences of welfarism have eaten deep into his morale and ambition. The old fierce pride and sensitive spirit of independence have died. In countless instances people who grew up in clean cabins, and whose parents would have starved before they would have asked for charity now shamelessly plot to 'get by' on public assistance of one kind or another. Two decades of uninspired welfarism have induced the belief that control of his destiny is in other hands (Caudill 1962:350, 389).

Nathan Glazer believes that the roots of the "culture of poverty" lie less in real poverty or deprivation than in dependency and the loss of self-reliance. It is still too early, however, to know what the full effect of welfare will be on the Travellers.

CHAPTER FIVE

The Urban Camp:
Managing Uncertainty

Because of the restricted number of camping sites available in urban areas, the population of most camps is considerably larger than the traditional travel unit of two or three families. The average size of Dublin camps is 6.4 families, and there are four sites in the city with more than twenty-five families each. Travellers who once camped primarily with relatives now find themselves in close proximity to "strangers"—families from other parts of the country with whom they are unfamiliar. For example, the three major kin groups at Holylands—the McDonaghs, Driscolls, and Briens—come from the West, the Midlands, and the Southeast, respectively. In such large and heterogeneous camps there is considerable tension and uncertainty. This chapter examines the ways in which Tinkers are adapting to this new social environment.

Uncertainty and Social Control

Because Tinkers traditionally lived in small groups of close kinsmen, they never developed formal mechanisms of social control or internal political organization. Within a lineage, the only recognized authority was that of the patriarch, and in his absence the eldest son; even that authority was accorded primarily as a sign of respect and carried little power. Both then and now, the itinerant population resembles what Honigman (1968), Balikci (1968), and others have described as an "atomistic" society: a society in which the nuclear family represents the major structural unit and the only formal social entity.

Interpersonal relations in such a highly individualistic environment tend to be characterized by uncertainty and ambivalence. As Rubel and Kupferer suggest:

> In societies in which the nuclear family is the unit of overriding significance, and in which children are socialized to see the family as the sole group upon which one can rely, the resultant incongruity—between those expectations and a realistic need to cope successfully with a larger, more complex world—is associated with a prominence of contention, wariness, and invidiousness in relationships outside the nuclear family (1968:190).

Although there is little doubt that Travellers have always been wary and suspicious in their dealings with others, given both their outcast status and their mobility, the large size of camps and the propinquity of unrelated families in urban areas has greatly heightened this uncertainty. Trouble or conflict is viewed as being latent in every social situation.

Travellers also lack an external source of social control to which they can turn. The police are quick to protect settled folk from Tinkers, but they do little to protect Tinkers from one another. The implicit policy of many Dublin police stations is not to respond to disturbances within Tinker camps, as long as nearby residents are not being affected, or to become involved in other ways in the internal affairs of the itinerant community. For their part, Travellers are also reluctant to contact the police, their traditional adversary.

The lack of privacy in large urban camps makes avoiding unwanted social interaction difficult; this, in turn, places additional strains on interpersonal relations. On official sites the huts are so close together that a conversation in one often may be overheard in the next. The large numbers of children and their practice of entering the homes of others at will makes it difficult for families to obtain any degree of privacy. Even adults rarely knock, but merely announce their presence as they enter. Hence the Traveller's own home offers no sanctuary or escape from others. Lacking space inside their huts or caravans and accustomed to living out-of-doors, families eat their meals and have conversations and arguments under the constant gaze of other families. Several families in Cork refused to occupy a new site until a fence, high

Plate 13.   Close-up of *Tigins* and overcrowding at another official site, Avila Park, Dublin. (*Photo by author*)

shrubbery, or some other barrier was placed between the huts, which had been built only fifteen feet apart, to provide some degree of privacy.

The unequal size or strength of Tinker kin groups in the city also contributes to uncertainty and tension. Some families in Dublin have many kinsmen living nearby on whom they may rely in case of trouble, but other families have few. Their relatives may be as far away as England, or they may still be travelling in the countryside. Because force and violence—or their threat—have always been the most important deterrents to antisocial behavior among Travellers, and the ultimate means of social control, families who have only a small number of kinsmen living in the city are at a distinct disadvantage.

A saying once popular in the countryside, "Strike one tinker and you strike the whole clan," does not necessarily hold true in

the city. An example may illustrate. The Briens, the most powerful group at Holylands, had a reputation for being tough. There
were six families in all—mother and father and their five married
sons. The Quilligans, in contrast, were alone; they had only recently returned to Ireland, leaving their relatives behind in England.
When the local ISC decided to stop renting trailers and sell them
to Holylanders at a greatly reduced price, "Old Jim" Brien immediately purchased his own trailer—and quickly shoved an additional
ten pounds into the ISC chairman's pocket as a down payment on
the Quilligans' trailer. He explained that the Quilligans were planning to return to England and did not wish to buy their trailer.
In fact, they had no such plans. When they returned to camp
that afternoon, Old Jim simply informed them that the chairman
had sold their trailer to him, flashing a receipt to prove it. Without kinsmen to support them, the Quilligans were unable to contest
his action and were forced to move out of their trailer.

The ultimate solution to the conflict, or its ever-present threat
in most Tinker camps, is to live alone. The nine or ten families
in Dublin who do pursue a solitary existence tend to be families
without strong kin ties in the city, who purposely avoid larger
camps "for the sake of peace." The mother of one such family
remarked with some bitterness:

> These days Travellin' People do be actin' more like animals than
> people. With all the black-guardin' and drinkin' you can't get a
> day's peace livin' on the same green with 'em. We do be lonesome
> here but I'd rather have it. It's best for me nerves (Mary Hand,
> age 50).

Interpersonal Relations

How do Tinkers deal with uncertainty? What social devices
do they use to smooth interaction with others in an environment
where interpersonal relations are ambivalent and often tense? The
behavior patterns described in the following pages are not unique
to urban Travellers. Rather, they are best viewed as intensified
versions of traditional responses. As social outcasts and nomads,
the Tinkers' social environment has always been characterized by
a degree of uncertainty.

Among Travellers, the word *friend* literally means "close kinsmen."[1] No concept of friendship comparable to that in the settled community exists outside the kinship network. Although there is a great deal of casual sociability in urban camps—Travellers spend many hours each day talking, gossiping, and joking with others—most interaction takes place on a superficial level. Individuals rarely discuss their true feelings or problems or express controversial opinions. There is even a reluctance to disagree with others. Hence what individuals say often bears no relationship to what they are actually thinking, but is calculated to accord with the opinions of others. Travellers often say, "Never let another man know your mind." One woman explains:

> What you tell a person in secret today, they'll be usin' against you tomorrow. It's best to tell them nothin' because you never know when they'll turn on you (Margaret Brien, age 32).

Similarly, another woman commented:

> You have to be careful what you say because Travellers is always castin' around for things to use against you. They try to bait you, to make you say things you'll be sorry for (Maggie McDonagh, age 50).

Travellers attempt to avoid involvement in social situations which could lead to trouble in other ways. They rarely say anything to an individual who is engaged in annoying or disruptive behavior. In public, they will tolerate almost any annoyance rather than risk offending or angering the individual responsible. This pattern extends even to the children. Undisciplined children are often bothersome and at times quite destructive. Young boys may beg for food and cigarettes, interrupt conversations, run off with tools, damage property, and so forth. Yet adults unrelated to them rarely scold or reprimand. They can afford to be blunt only if the child is related to them; if not, they prefer to ignore the annoyance rather than risk antagonizing the child's parents.

---

[1] The term *friend* was also used among the Irish peasantry to refer to kinsmen (Arensberg and Kimball 1940).

This tolerance is most pronounced in families that are "weak"— lacking in kin support or otherwise unable to defend themselves. For example, several Brien children burned down a wooden outdoor toilet. The toilet was located near the camps of the Driscoll and McDonagh families. Yet although a group of adults from these two kin groups observed the children start the fire, they made no attempt to interfere.

Travellers frequently use children as intermediaries in dealings with other families in order to avoid conflict. When any favor such as a small loan or a ride to the hospital or pub is needed, a child is sent to make the request. This enables the adults to avoid embarrassing refusals and otherwise awkward or compromising situations. At one point Tom was troubled by the fact that Franci had let two weeks pass without repaying the five pounds he had borrowed. In need of money to go to the pub, but not wanting to offend Franci or reveal that he was short of cash, Tom sent his daughter to ask him politely if he "remembered" the five pounds. In this transaction—in which the money was both borrowed and returned through a child—the men saved face and neither compromised his position.

In order to establish some sense of security in interpersonal relations, Tinkers often trace out their genealogies with other families in search of common relatives. A kinship tie, no matter how distant, can serve as a basis for friendship and cooperation. Also, attributing a relationship to kinship gives it structural support and a sense of durability. After Nan Driscoll and Margaret Brien discovered a very distant link—Nan's mother's mother's brother had married Margaret's father's mother's sister—they often reminded one another of their common tie, exaggerating the degree of its closeness. This kinship link formed the basis for a friendship of sorts between the two women and a quasi-alliance between their two families which lasted for the duration of their stay at Holylands.

The use of distant kin ties as a means of ensuring smooth social interaction became especially apparent to me while accompanying one informant on several horse-buying trips outside Dublin. With each group of Travellers we met with whom there existed some possibility of a kin tie, he began reconstructing his family history as far back as he could remember. When a common relative was discovered, social relations between the individuals were suddenly on much firmer ground.

The exchange of small gifts between families is another device Tinkers use to temper social relations. Gifts of cigarettes, drink, and clothing obtained through begging and favors such as offering rides and bringing back someone else's wandering horses are often exchanged between families. The pattern of exchange, in which the weaker, more vulnerable families more frequently give gifts to members of stronger families, reveals a purpose beyond simple reciprocity in kind. Gift-giving is often a sort of bribery: people give small gifts or perform favors in order to remain on the "good side" of others. For example, in one week two children were born to Holylands women, one to a Brien from the dominant group in camp and one to a Driscoll from a weaker kin group. By custom, Tinkers are expected to *hansel* the baby— to give a silver coin to the newborn for luck. Several of the McDonaghs, the third kin group at Holylands, gave fifty pence coins to the Brien child, despite the fact that they were often at odds with the Briens and did not like the child's parents. Each gave only a ten pence coin to the Driscoll child.

Families in urban camps take a keen interest in the activities of others, and gossip is rife. Whenever a lorry drives into Holylands, adults get up to see who it is and where they are going. Children are encouraged to report information about others to their parents. Because of their easy access to the campfires and shelters of other families, children are often privy to information their parents could not obtain. As one woman remarked, "The children here is the ears of their parents." Such information or gossip is, in turn, spread through each individual's personal network to others in camp and, in visiting, to other Travellers in the city.

A pervasive pattern of gossip is often cited as evidence of suspicion and contentiousness in interpersonal relations. Upon closer examination, gossip can also be seen to have adaptive functions (see Gluckman 1963). In a setting where little information is volunteered, gossip is the primary means of learning about other families, not only in one's own camp but throughout the city. In this way gossip increases an individual's familiarity with other Tinkers, thereby reducing uncertainty in social relations. As Swezd (1966) notes, the flow of information from gossip helps provide the individual with facts on which to act. An example may illustrate. Three new families, whom most of the families at

Holylands had never personally met, moved into camp from the
north side of the city. Through gossip it was learned that these
families were "rough" and that one of the men was especially
violent. On the basis of this information, Holylanders knew how
to handle the "strangers" before they arrived. One man, for example, moved his pile of scrap metal to fill in a large open area
between his shelter and that of the neighboring family in order
to prevent the newcomers from making camp next to him.

Gossip may also serve as an instrument for censuring deviant
behavior. Since a Traveller cannot tell another adult directly that
he is misbehaving without inciting hostility, disapproval is expressed through gossip—in the words of Gluckman, in "behind the
back tattle." Thus a troublesome individual can be sanctioned on
a covert level, while overtly a show of friendship and harmony is
maintained.

Teasing and the playing of practical jokes is especially common
among Tinker men and often serves to dissipate tension in interpersonal relations. As Radcliffe-Brown (1952) noted in his classic
essay on the subject, joking involves a "peculiar combination of
friendliness and antagonism." Much of Traveller joking, called
"slagging," has a ritual quality. It is a kind of duel fought with
verbal insults in which each man tries to best his opponent by
making the wittiest and most telling remarks. The insults used
often refer to some personal weakness or idiosyncracy. Red Ned,
for example, is teased about his red hair and flushed face; another
man is ridiculed for using black shoe polish to conceal his grey
hair. Joking is also the means by which Travellers communicate
dissatisfaction and specific complaints that cannot be voiced seriously without creating hostility. Red Ned, camped next to the
road leading into Holylands, was disturbed by the recurrent reckless driving of another man. Even though he feared that one of
his children would eventually be struck, he hesitated to complain
directly. Instead, at the pub one evening he manipulated the conversation onto the topic of driving and then proceeded in a joking
fashion to mimic the Traveller who sped down the road with children fleeing in every direction. Through joking, Red Ned voiced
his complaint, but in a manner which did not place the other man
in a position where he felt threatened or compelled to defend
himself.

Practical jokes or pranks often serve the same purposes. Mocky Tom gave up the drink in order to save money, but he continued to go to the pub each evening with his drinking companions, ordering bottled lemonade. One night while he was in the restroom his companions dropped half a dozen laxative pills in his lemonade. Clearly this prank (which imposed a slight physical indignity on the victim the following day as he made frequent trips to the bushes) was a way in which his companions were able to negatively sanction Mocky Tom's attempt to save money while they freely spent theirs on drink.

In an environment in which people are generally not trusted and strong social contacts are absent, it is important for men to establish a reputation for being tough. One way this is accomplished is through roughhousing, which may take the form of wrestling, sparring, and even stick-fighting. This activity is done in a friendly fashion, but it is serious in that the way a man handles himself—how aggressively he fights, how much punishment he can withstand, and how quickly he gives in—is observed by others in camp. Largely as a result of this aggressive play, a consensus is reached as to who are the toughest men and therefore to be treated with respect, and who are the weakest and therefore vulnerable to being taken advantage of. Of course the size and strength of a man's kin group backing him up is also important.

The value of being tough is learned at an early age.[2] Fathers often playfully slap around and box their young sons to "toughen" them, and boys who cry upon hurting themselves are not consoled

---

[2] Walter Miller, who describes "toughness" as a "focal concern" of lower-class American males, suggests one explanation for this syndrome: ". . . a significant proportion of lower class males are reared in a predominantly female household, and lack of consistently present male figure with whom to identify and from whom to learn essential components of 'male' role. Since women serve as a primary object of identification during pre-adolescent years, the almost obsessive lower class concern with 'masculinity' probably resembles a type of compulsive-reaction-formation" (Miller 1965:339). Although many Traveller households are now becoming female-dominated, this has not been the case in the past. Moreover, even in the few households in which fathers are absent, there are many other adult men in the camp who provide models of male roles for boys to emulate.

but often shamed into "acting like men." Boys are encouraged to stand up to others and never to run from a fight unless badly outmatched. When ten-year-old Brendan was beaten up by another boy at Holylands, his mother encouraged him to "get his own back" and gave him a few elementary lessons in boxing. Several weeks later he got into another scuffle with the same boy and soundly defeated him. He gave his mother an almost blow-by-blow description of the fight, upon which she rewarded him with ten shillings.

Many of the interactions just discussed, such as the pervasive gossip and the practical joke played on the individual who wanted to stop drinking, can also be viewed as levelling mechanisms. They are social devices used to pull down individuals who attempt to get above the common level of the group. Of the many writers who have discussed levelling mechanisms, most have examined their role in evening out social and economic disparities between members of a community (e.g. Foster 1967). But how might levelling mechanisms be adaptive in reducing uncertainty and tension in social relations? In a study of migrant labor camps in the United States, where the unstructured and unpredictable social environment is somewhat similar to that of large Traveller camps, Nelkin suggests:

> To reduce the potentialities for misunderstandings under these circumstances, there is a tendency in the camps to minimize the differences between participants; to bring people to a common level (1969:381).

A certain sense of security is attained in a group in which all individuals live at the same level, with few differences in wealth or prestige. In an environment in which economic opportunities are limited, it is disturbing to others to see one individual get above the rest. Such an individual threatens the self-esteem of those who have not achieved the same degree of success. When one Traveller goes off the drink, for example, the others must ask themselves, "Why can't I do the same?"

Although levelling mechanisms most frequently take the form of gossip, Travellers in some instances resort to more forceful actions. Martin Brien, who was hired by a local ISC to drive the school minibus to pick up Tinker children from nearby camps each morning, is a case in point. Martin's peers not only resented his mobility aspirations but lamented the fact that he and not they had been the one to receive this prized job. At first there was malicious gossip, including accusations that Martin was informing settlement committee members of the smuggling activities some residents of his camp were engaged in. Next the bus was sabotaged—the tires were deflated and the gasoline tank emptied—making Martin disrupt the school schedule by picking the children up late. Subsequently, the side mirrors were broken off the bus and one side was badly scratched. Martin finally quit when some parents began keeping their children inside when he arrived, forcing him to fetch each child individually. To the pleasure of those who had not qualified for the job, it was finally given to a settled person.

Individuals who accumulate more wealth than others in their camp often seek to neutralize the invidiousness of others by sharing part of their fortune. When Michael Driscoll received his first paycheck from a job with an office-cleaning firm, he spent part of it on Guinness stout, which he made a great display of sharing with those sitting around the campfire that night. Similarly, Paddy McDonagh, whose family's income of approximately forty-five pounds per week placed them well above other Holylanders, sought to maintain friendly relations by regularly chauffeuring others, particularly the Briens, to the pubs, cinemas, hospitals, or wherever they wished to go.

Drinking as an Adaptive Response

Drinking among Tinkers has greatly increased in the city. Travellers have always been heavy drinkers, but in the past few families had enough cash to drink regularly, and most consumption was confined to periodic binges. Today, much of the Travellers' increased income in the city goes for drink; many families spend half or more of their weekly earnings, or about fifteen pounds, in the pubs. Most men drink from five to seven days a week, consuming six to eight pints of stout each night and often double that amount for two or three days after receiving the dole. Drinking among women is more sporadic; when they accompany their

husbands to the pubs they generally drink half as much as the
men. It is customary for men to order half-pints of stout for
their wives with each pint they purchase for themselves. Most
drinking occurs in the pub, with the exception of "rough" Tinkers
who, because of their especially dirty and rugged appearance, are
generally not admitted to pubs and must therefore drink outside
on the sidewalk. When pubs close at 11:30 P.M., it is not uncommon for men to buy several more pints of stout to take back to
camp. On some evenings groups of men and women sit around
the campfire drinking until two or three o'clock in the morning.
Although there are few restraints on overindulgence, complete
stupor is neither the desired goal nor the usual outcome of Tinker
drinking.

From the perspective of the settled community, drinking
among Travellers constitutes a major social problem. It is viewed
as an unnecessary waste of money leading some families into
destitution as well as a major public nuisance. Tinkers, who com-
prise less than 1 percent of the total Irish population, account
for 35 percent of the total number of persons imprisoned for
drunkenness.[3] There is little question that drinking exacts a heavy
toll on the Traveller community. The immediate concern of this
section, however, is to examine excessive drinking not as a Traveller problem per se, but as a response to their social environment.

Drinking is an effective social lubricant. By the third or
fourth pint of stout Travellers begin to relax, conversation becomes more animated, and many of the barriers that normally
exist between individuals begin to disappear. With this loosening
of inhibitions, there is an initial increase in sociability and group
activities, such as card playing, storytelling, ballad singing, and
occasionally step-dancing. It is not the alcohol alone that affects
behavior but the situation itself, for Tinker drinking sessions are
culturally defined as occasions during which people may talk and
act with relative impunity. Drinking is a "time out" from many
of the otherwise imperative norms of everyday life (cf. MacAndrew

---

[3]The Tinkers' position as outcasts, their high visibility, and the tendency
of some to drink on sidewalks and in other public places accounts for part
of this excessive percentage. Statistics were obtained from the Department
of Justice.

and Edgerton 1969). Under the influence of drink, for example, men and women often engage in bawdy sexual joking which in most other contexts would be regarded as "scandalous" behavior.

Alcohol and the drinking session provide an outlet and excuse for the release of pent-up grievances and hostilities. Antagonistic behavior is often excused with such comments as, "the drink made him do it" or, "it's the drink talkin'."

Frequent and heavy drinking is also a response to the boredom which has become so commonplace. In the past, most men's idle hours were spent making extra tinware, carving clothes pegs or wooden flowers, tending the horses, or setting and checking rabbit snares. Today these activities no longer exist. In the city men have very little to occupy their time apart from a few hours of scavenging each day. Consequently drinking, along with games played in the pub such as darts and cards, has become an important pastime and a major antidote to boredom. It is not uncommon for men to sit around the campfire for several hours waiting until they can leave for the pub. Particularly in winter, the pub also offers refuge from dark, drafty, and overcrowded shelters, and from the demands of children.

Excessive drinking among some men must also be viewed as a reaction to the insecurity and low self-esteem arising from their pariah status in Irish society. Travellers have always been regarded as outcasts by settled folk and treated with suspicion and disdain. But since the obsolescence of their traditional trades, their position has further eroded. The romantic image of Travellers as carefree, adventuresome vagabonds, reflected in some of the literature of the settled community (cf. Synge 1907, 1912; Stephens 1914; Clifford 1951; and MacMahon 1967), has changed. Travellers are now viewed, at best, as objects of charity and pity; at worst they are seen as a noxious social problem. Travellers, of course, become aware of these stereotypes through their interactions with settled folk. As one Traveller commented about Dubliners:

> The people in the houses don't even call us Travellers or Tinkers no more, but just plain 'itinerants.' Some calls us the 'itinerant problem.' Half the Travellin' People don't know what itinerant means (Mick Driscoll, age 60).

As will be discussed in the following chapter, low self-esteem among men has been compounded by their declining role within the family.

Like other minority groups whose traditional behavior patterns are changing and like the materially deprived in many cultures, Travellers seek and find relief from their psychic pain in alcohol. Among North American Indians, for example, Graves notes:

> Unhappily, drunkenness has come to occupy a prominent place in the adaptive repertoire of both reservation and urban Indians: its narcotizing effects are leaned on heavily as a way of coping with feelings of personal inadequacy and failure by temporarily escaping from them (1971:305).

It is in the pub that a male proves himself as a man.

In sum, drinking helps Tinkers cope with their social environment. It is clearly adaptive in that it promotes communication and the expression of grievances that are impossible to reveal in other social contexts. It is also one of the few recreational activities open to itinerants, and in this capacity is an important remedy for boredom. And at another level, it offers temporary escape from feelings of inadequacy and insecurity.

In the long run, however, it is maladaptive. With one-half of most families' income spent on alcohol, drinking represents an extravagant waste of capital which is sorely needed for better shelter, food, and conveniences. Excessive drinking also has serious consequences for the health of individual Travellers. A number of Holylands men evidence alcohol-related mental and physical disturbances, including guilt feelings, loss of appetite, and in more serious cases, the "shakes." And although alcohol and the drinking session are socially integrative, chronic excessive drinking leading to alcoholism impairs an individual's ability to relate to others, particularly to members of his own family (Kessel and Walton 1965). Hence in the long term, excessive reliance on drinking as a coping response constitutes a vicious circle in which the original conditions—ambivalent social relations, low self-esteem, and feelings of insecurity—are worsened.

Some Tinkers are aware of the costs of overindulgence and often denounce drinking. On many occasions I heard men remark, "Drinking is the ruination of the Travellin' People" and, "Drink is a cancer." From awareness of this and from a desire to spend less money, many adults take measures to cut down their alcohol consumption. Men often take "the pledge"—a sworn oath before a priest not to drink or to drink no more than two pints of stout each day for a specified period of time, usually three months. Other tactics include going to the pub an hour later than usual, taking only enough cash to purchase a certain number of pints, and filling up on soft drinks before buying the first pint of stout. The importance of drinking as a coping device is evidenced by the failure of most attempts to abstain. During my fieldwork at least ten men at Holylands took the pledge, but only one lasted the full three months.

The group also exerts strong pressures (levelling mechanisms) on abstaining individuals, making it difficult for them to stop drinking or to drink only moderately. As Graves notes:

> Once group drunkenness becomes a normative pattern it serves as a standard of behavior even for those participants who may not have the same psychological needs that generated the pattern in the first place (1971:302).

Shifting as an Adaptive Response

In the past, "shifting" or moving to a new camp was necessary mainly because the demand for the Tinkers' crafts and services was not great enough in a single area to permit permanent residence. In contrast, Travellers' present-day occupations in urban areas do not require the same mobility. In fact the profits from begging and scavenging may increase with sedentarism. By remaining in one area, a beggar becomes known to local residents and increases her chances of developing patroness-client relationships. And as Traveller women become familiar with the representatives and policies of local charity organizations, they learn how to use them more effectively. There is also a tendency on the part of both charities and householders to help those Travellers who have been in their area the longest. Newcomers are always regarded with an extra degree of caution and mistrust. Similarly, the scavenger who knows the local territory—the houses and businesses most likely to have scrap and the personalities of the individuals he must deal with—enjoys an advantage.

Plate 14. Shifting to a new camp in Dublin. (*Photo by author*)

Despite such benefits, few families are truly sedentary. The amount of movement or shifting varies a great deal: many families shift about once a month, others only three or four times a year, and a few may remain in the same location for several years if allowed to do so. Mobility is highest among families in unauthorized camps (roadsides, empty lots, and fields) and lowest among those living in full-serviced official or local authority sites. One reason for this difference is the absence of trash or garbage removal services in unofficial camps. After a few months garbage accumulates, the camp is strewn with litter, and the surrounding hedgerows—used for toilet purposes—are despoiled. Under such conditions rats often become a problem. On official sites with toilets and trash collection, these problems are reduced considerably. Additional amenities available on the official sites are also an inducement to remain settled. A family moving back onto the roadside or into an open field would have to do without running water and electricity.

Nevertheless, the turnover on official sites is considerable. At the three largest sites in Dublin, more than one-fourth of the residents left during 1975. At Holylands, which has far fewer facilities, thirty-seven families resided there during my first fieldwork; only eight families remained for the entire year. The reasons for shifting obviously go beyond mere considerations of garbage and amenities.

What motivates Travellers to shift? How does shifting help them cope with their environment? As previously mentioned, fission, the breaking away of antagonistic parties, has always been a primary means of resolving conflict among Tinkers. The decision to leave the group is a pragmatic one taken to avoid further trouble. In responses to a questionnaire sent to all Itinerant Settlement Committees in 1972, a majority indicated that "fighting" or "conflict between families" was the single most important cause for Travellers leaving local sites. In large camps such as Holylands, families often move first to different locations within the camp in order to escape interpersonal tensions.

The following example illustrates the use of shifting as a response to conflict. When John Driscoll first arrived at Holylands in the autumn, he set up camp next to his parents and married brothers. Soon relations between his wife and his mother became strained, and they argued frequently. At the insistence of his wife, John moved off the asphalt strip and into the field at the center of Holylands. The family remained there until the continuous flow of water from a broken tap swamped the area. They then shifted to the far end of the site, next to the McDonaghs. They were there several months when Luke McDonagh began suspecting that someone was stealing from his scrap pile and secretly blamed John. Relations between the men became tense, and during a drinking binge a fight occurred in which John soundly defeated his accuser. The next day both men and their immediate families left Holylands. John left because he felt he could not find "peace" anywhere in the camp, and Luke left because of the disgraceful beating he received in a fight he had instigated.

When disputes between rival kin groups break out or when fighting appears imminent, families who are outnumbered by their opponents tend to shift closer to kinsmen in order to strengthen their position. The Cashes threatened to retaliate against the Caseys after two of their relatives were killed in an automobile crash caused by the reckless and drunken driving of Tom Casey. Within a few days after the treats had been made, several Casey families moved to the same camp for protection.

Shifting is also a common response to personal problems. Upon the death of a family member, the surviving relatives invariably move away to escape the memories the former camp evokes. A week prior to my arrival at Holylands, twelve families had left the camp within two days of the accidental death of a relative. One family left Holylands after the husband had taken the pledge in order to avoid strong group pressures to resume drinking. And as will be discussed in the following chapter, when parents suspect that a daughter is courting or becoming involved with a boy, they very often move away to terminate the relationship.

A family may leave a camp simply to avoid embarassment or loss of status. The following is a rather unique case, but it does indicate the extent to which Travellers resort to shifting in an effort to save face. Alice Browne had been the prize pupil at St. Kieran's, a special school for Traveller children. Upon graduation, the headmistress enrolled Alice in grace seven in the regular National School system. Dublin newspapers carried the story of her success and with some overstatement described her as the first itinerant child to reach secondary school level. In the camp there was much invidious gossip about Alice's family and achievement, including claims that she had done well only because she was competing with other Traveller children rather than with settled children. Within the first weeks of the new school term it became apparent that the training Alice had received at the Traveller school had not adequately prepared her for secondary school. Frustrated and uncomfortable in her new setting, she dropped out. Almost immediately, giving the excuse that they were going to Northern Ireland to have a new barrel-top wagon made, her family left Dublin and its gossip network entirely.

Shifting is frequently the means by which Tinkers attempt to dodge police and court summonses. In the city Travellers are often cited for traffic offenses, usually for not having a valid driver's license or registration; also, as previously mentioned they are often fined for permitting their horses to wander. Because of frequent shifting, many Dublin police find it so difficult to serve Tinkers with summonses for traffic violations that they are reluctant to issue them. One patrolman privately admitted that he was instructed by his superior not to ticket Travellers, because they were so difficult to track down and because they spoiled the department's "statistics."

Where serious offenses such as theft are involved, Travellers may leave Ireland altogether. Sixteen-year-old Mickalo broke into a local community center and stole an assortment of items including cutlery, dinner plates, and a flashlight. His parents learned of the deed several days later when Mickalo was attempting to sell the goods to another family. With Mickalo already on probation for a similar offense and fearful that he might receive a jail sentence, his parents put him on a boat to Liverpool and ultimately to Manchester to stay with relatives. After a number of months in England, the offender usually returns to Ireland under a different name. Since Tinkers possess no identification and most are unable to sign their names, it is almost impossible for authorities to trace them.

Last, moving to a new location is often a response to boredom. Without an occasional change in environment Tinkers become bored and often depressed. In fact, the absence of change is a major problem Tinkers encounter in adapting to housing. The activities involved in packing up the gear, making the move, and setting up a new camp seem to be therapy for boredom. A new setting also provides a much-needed visual change; as Tinkers often say, "You get tired looking at the one place all the time."

The need for change is often felt most acutely after the long, gloomy winter. Inspired by good weather and nostalgia for clean air, lush plant life, and the beauty of the countryside, some Dublin families leave the city for several months each summer. Some return to the countryside to camp with relatives; others merely move to the wooded outskirts of the city. In 1975, for example, ten families at Labre Park paid their rent in advance, left their *tigins*, and moved into tents and wagons in nearby rural areas for the summer. The desire for change carries over to material possessions. Travellers seldom keep articles for more than a few months before discarding them or swapping them to someone else.

When most Dublin Travellers shift, they do not go far. Many families who left Holylands moved to roadside camps less than a mile away. In several instances families shifted just two blocks to a large grassy verge adjoining a nearby convent. The principal reasons for this are the economic considerations discussed earlier. Once a family has become established and has acquired good begging and scavenging contacts, it is disadvantageous to move away. Moreover many families, unless shifting in a large group or moving into the camp of kinsmen, are insecure about moving into a new area where they are unfamiliar with the local families. And some families who have children enrolled in school do not wish to disrupt their education by shifting out of the area covered by the local ISC school bus service.

Clearly, shifting offers a quick resolution to a variety of short-range problems. Like drinking, however, it also incurs long-range costs. By prohibiting continuity of association among various families, shifting undermines social relationships. As Jacobsen (1971, 1973) and others note, friendship and trust are founded upon reciprocity. But reciprocity requires a positive expectation of future interaction. Each party to a social relationship must have confidence in the other's capacity and responsibility for meeting, at a future time, his obligation to the relationship. And as long as Tinkers continue to shift and remain unsettled, this guarantee does not exist. Also, negative sanctions such as gossip and ridicule lose some of their effectiveness in a mobile population where individuals can escape opprobrium simply by leaving the area. Thus shifting solves many short-range problems, but in the end it heightens uncertainty and ambivalence in social relations.

CHAPTER SIX

Family and Marriage in the City

The new social environment of the urban camp and the economic adaptation Tinkers have made in the city have brought about important changes in marriage and family patterns. This chapter discusses some of these changes and examines their adaptive significance.

Sex Roles and Power

Perhaps the most apparent change in the urban Traveller family has been the shift in sex roles, specifically the increasing independence of women and the concomitant decline in the male's authority in the family. Through begging and welfare, many women now provide most of their family's daily subsistence, whereas men contribute comparatively little, spending their income instead on entertainment (mostly drink) and occasional major purchases such as a lorry, caravan, or horse.[1] With their enhanced economic role, Tinker women are becoming more assertive and are demanding a greater voice in decisions affecting the family. As LeVine (1965), Blood and Wolfe (1960), and others have shown, a change

---

[1]One notable exception to this pattern is the minority of prosperous families in which the men, mostly asphalt layers and roadside traders, earn a substantial income; the women in many of these families do not beg. These men are active, and because of their prosperity they have high self-esteem relative to other Travellers.

in the role of family provider (the one who contributes the greater
resources to the family) usually results in a corresponding shift in
power. Following Stephens, power is here defined loosely as a
matter of ". . . who dominates, who submits; who makes the
family decisions—husband, wife, or both jointly; who gets his or
her way in case of disagreements and who commands and who
obeys" (1963:296). There is no doubt that Traveller women
are gaining power.

> Today the Travellin' women is gettin' very bold, and what makes them
> so bold is that they're under no compliment to the men now that
> they're doin' most of the work beggin' (Nan Driscoll, age 56).

In the past, Traveller society was strongly patriarchal
(MacGreine 1931). Men made all the major decisions and con-
trolled the family's finances. As one woman recalled with some
dramatic exaggeration:

> A woman would be afeard to hide a hay-penny for herself, because
> if the man heard it rattlin' in her pocket she might get kilt over it
> (Biddy Brien, age 74).

Wife-beating was not uncommon. By all accounts, men seem to
have regarded women as chattel. Sampson (1891), Arnold (1898),
Synge (1912), and MacRitchie (1889) cite instances of wife-swapping
among Travellers. MacRitchie, for example, cites an instance in
which a Tinker who desired another man's prize horse swapped his
young, attractive wife for the coveted animal plus the owner's "ugly
old wife" (1889:352). In writing about Tinkers and Gypsies, however, authors have frequently embellished the facts and it is not
uncommon for Travellers to fabricate such stories.

Examples of the increased independence and decision-making
power of Traveller women today are numerous. Most women no
longer turn over their earnings to their husband automatically.
In fact, many now keep separate savings. Some Traveller men
must now borrow money from their wives when their own cash
runs out. Having spent his own money at the pub, for example,
Grey Tom was forced to ask his wife for a ten-pound loan in order
to repair his lorry. She gave him the money, but only on the condition that he pay her one pound in interest. And in arranging

marriages for their children, women now have a stronger voice. In the past, men usually had the final decision in making a "match"; but in Dublin families today it is clearly a joint decision, with either spouse having the right to veto a match they disapprove of. Similarly, the decisions as to when to shift and where to camp are no longer made exclusively by the man. Following a dispute with another family at Holylands, Marty McDonagh decided to move to a new camp. Ignoring the objections of his wife, he loaded their goods into their wagon, hitched up the horse, and started to leave camp. But when it became apparent that his wife would not follow, he turned back and unpacked.

In dealing with Irish officials, especially social workers and welfare officers, women often represent the family. This pattern is reinforced by the fact that settled folk find Tinker women less intimidating than the men; therefore they routinely take matters directly to the women. One exception to this pattern is that it is the men who interact with the police. The role of the woman as family spokesman presents a marked contrast to the past, when it was primarily the man who dealt with the outside world.

Other factors besides the wife's enhanced economic role have weakened the husband's position. In the past, one of the primary responsibilities of Tinker men was caring for the family's means of transportation—maintaining the wagon or cart and looking after the animals—which in a nomadic society is extremely important. With increased sedentarism and the transition from horses to motor vehicles which do not require constant care, the importance of these responsibilities has waned.

It is difficult to assess to what extent men assisted in the care of children in the past, but according to some informants the father played an important part in educating his sons. Most significantly, he taught them the skills of the road—particularly tinsmithing and the crafting of a variety of domestic goods. Today these trades are gone, and scavenging does not require the same degree of instruction. Thus, men have lost not only their position as breadwinner, but also much of the satisfaction and reward which comes from fulfilling other familial roles. In a few Dublin families, men do little more than gather wood to keep the campfire going. Other domestic tasks such as cooking, cleaning, and washing are still considered women's work as they always have been. For a man to perform such duties would, in his eyes, diminish his masculinity. Thus the man's contribution to the daily operation of the household as well as to its income is very often minimal.

Today Tinker women, especially younger wives, are much less willing to tolerate abuses from their husbands than they were in the past. Indeed, many women strike back when they feel they have been wronged. Katie Brien refused to prepare any meals for her husband after he spent his dole money, including the three pounds he owed her, at the pub on drink. Another woman broke all the family's crockery and smashed her husband's accordian when she discovered he had left a pub with another woman.

> The women aren't so foolish as they used to be. Years ago the women was too soft and too honest. But now they've gone clever and they're more the bosses. They're able for the men. They're not scared of the men no more (Nan Driscoll, age 56).

One factor external to the itinerant community that encourages women to demand better treatment from their husbands is the influence of begging patronesses. Through contact with their "ladies," many women have become aware of an alternative model of conjugal relations—that of middle-or upper-class settled society. There women are not treated as inferiors (at least not so blatantly,) and are rarely beaten; decision-making is more equitably distributed between spouses. These differences may be either observed in the homes of patronesses or verbally communicated to Tinker women by their ladies. Moreover, encounters with patronesses also serve to transmit to Traveller women many of the negative attitudes settled folk hold toward Traveller men—whom they blame for wandering horses, trespassing, thievery, and other "itinerant" problems. At the same time, most patronesses show a great deal of sympathy for itinerant women and their children, whom they view as victims of repressive and irresponsible husbands. Thus settled folk often heighten the Tinker woman's awareness of the inequities and injustices which exist in her marriage. One man complained about his wife's patronesses, saying:

I don't know what those ladies in the houses are tellin' her, but
I don't like it. Everything is fine when she goes out [begging],
but when she comes back she's pure vexed with me for nothin'.
I haven't done nothin' (Red Ned Brien, age 32).

Changing attitudes among some young Traveller women about
family size and the use of family planning methods is another sign
of their increasing independence and of the influence of their
patronesses. Traveller families are exceptionally large—most households contain six or seven children. The Tinker fertility rate of
10.4 children per prolific woman over age forty is one of the highest recorded, surpassed only by the Hutterites (Crawford and
Gmelch 1974).[2] At Holylands, three women had each given birth
more than twenty times (of the sixty-five children born to them,
however, only forty-four survived childhood).[3]

Large families have always been highly valued by Travellers,
but particularly among the men, who see them as evidence of
their virility. Today there are also strong economic incentives,
since all major welfare benefits increase with the number of dependents. But to women, on whom most of the burdens of child
care fall, giving birth every year or two is often an unwelcome
hardship. Many women no longer desire such large families and
some claim to want only two or three children. Such views are
often inspired, or at least encouraged, by contact with their settled patronesses, many of whom recognize the need for some
form of family planning among itinerants (as well as settled society).

---

[2]This high fertility can be explained in part by the long reproductive
careers of the females, who marry young and continue reproducing until
they are forty or forty-five years of age.

[3]The infant mortality rate among Tinkers is exceptionally high. In the
1960 census of itinerants, 782 of 6904 children born alive died in the
first year of life—a mortality rate of 113 per thousand. This figure may
be compared with the national average of 30.5 per thousand (1961) and
a rate of 60 per thousand calculated for the lowest income group in Dublin.
Although I do not have exact figures, the infant mortality rate appears to
have dropped considerably in recent years as the Tinker's standard of living and access to medical care has improved.

The desire to limit family size is strongly opposed by most men and by some older, more traditional women. Nevertheless, some young women have made a conscious effort to avoid pregnancy. Two Holylands women were taking birth control pills obtained with the help of one of their patronesses. Two others had secretly gone to a family planning clinic to inquire about IUDs but became frightened and left before seeing a doctor.

The large number of Travellers camped together in urban areas also tends to bolster the woman's influence in the family. Many women in Dublin have relatives camped in the city or else nearby. Although a woman's relatives will not interfere in a normal marital dispute, this has some restraining effect on their husbands. The knowledge that some of his wife's relatives, particularly her brothers, are camped only a few miles away prevents many men from overly abusing their wives. Women, in turn, derive security from the knowledge that they have relatives to flee to. Consequently, they have less reason to fear their husbands and are more likely to take advantage of their increased economic independence. In the rural setting where women were isolated from their kinsmen, wife-beating was a very real threat and not one to be taken lightly.

Although it is clear that most women have become the heads of their households in terms of everyday functioning, it cannot be said that there has been a complete shift in power from husbands to wives. First, only a short time has elapsed since women began assuming economic responsibility in the family. And there is bound to be some lag before power relationships adjust fully to new economic realities, if they do at all. Second, as Stephens notes, power relationships are very difficult to assess accurately. "They are not neatly summarized into cultural rules . . . [and] . . .they tend to vary a great deal within the same society" (1963:296). Clearly the personalities of the spouses have a great deal to do with who makes the important decisions. In Traveller society, where physical force is often used to get one's way, the size and strength of the spouse is an important factor. Hefty, 250-pound Maggie McDonagh fractured her husband's nose and gave him eleven stitches across the forehead after he broke his pledge and went on a three-day drinking binge, abusing her and the children. Although women now have considerable independence in their own affairs and those of their children, they have little control over their husbands' activities. Outside the family, men still do as they wish. Few women have the authority to keep their husbands home at night or to make them contribute a greater share of their income to family expenses.

Instability and Conflict

Most Tinker marriages in Dublin are characterized by a good deal of suspicion, mistrust, jealousy, quarreling, and sometimes open fighting. There is little doubt that the dislocation of traditional sex roles, notably the failure of men to contribute much to the daily subsistence of the family, has strained relations between many husbands and wives. At Holylands men and women often view one another as separate and opposing interest groups.

Plate 15.   Family life at Holylands, Dublin. *(Photo by Pat Langan)*

Women complain that they must work unremittingly to meet the family's subsistence needs, while their husbands do little but drink, gamble, go to the movies, and collect "the odd bit of scrap." The laziness of men is a frequent topic of conversation among women. Nan Driscoll complained:

> When me old man gets his money he goes off to the pubs with his friends and drinks. And he forgets his family. He never buys the kids a package of sweets or a bar of chocolate. He doesn't want to know them when he has money. But when he's broke, he comes back saying he's very hungry, wanting us to feed him. We give him something to eat and he's real nice for awhile, until he gets more money of his own.

The strain in the marital bond is also reflected in jealousy and mistrust between many spouses. Husbands are particularly suspicious of their wives having extramarital affairs and attempt to keep a close watch on their activities. Some men at Holylands prohibit their wives from visiting after dark with families at the opposite end of camp, where they cannot be observed. While alone, a woman must never talk to another man, except perhaps a close kinsman. Some husbands take their wives with them whenever they leave camp at night. Some even discourage their wives from wearing clothing which is too respectable and otherwise "prettying" themselves in a way that might be attractive to other men. Several informants expressed the view that an attractive woman is a liability in a marriage because she causes too much jealousy. Mick Driscoll objected to a proposed match for his son on the grounds that the girl was too attractive and would bring the boy "a life of misery."

To some degree, Travellers have always been jealous spouses. In 1931 MacGreine wrote:

> Married women are not allowed to make any freedom with men other than close blood relations of their own or their husband. Should a husband find that his wife was seen drinking with another man, or being friendly with him, he will undoubtedly give her a good thrashing. Husbands are undoubtedly very jealous of their wives and will not deny the fact (1931:176).

But in the rural setting there were few opportunities for extra-marital affairs—groups were small and isolated, and so women were easily supervised. In the urban milieu, however, these constraints are absent. The size of urban camps and the close proximity of unrelated families makes close supervision difficult. Women who are away from camp most of the day begging come into frequent contact with other Travellers. Furthermore, there are opportunities for secret liaisons with other men within camp at night.

Although such opportunities exist, adultery on the part of Traveller women is not common. The jealousy of males is based largely on their own feelings of inadequacy, arising from their diminished economic role and from their exaggerated conception of the freedom women have in the city. Gerry Brien left Holylands to visit a sick relative in Wexford. He had planned to be away several days but returned the following evening, suspecting that his wife might be having an affair in his absence. As he admitted later, he had no reason for suspicion other than the fact that his wife was alone and unsupervised.

The suspicion and tension that exist in many marriages cause frequent quarreling and, occasionally, physical violence. During the first period of fieldwork at Holylands, approximately fifty arguments in which husbands and wives exchanged physical blows were either witnessed or overheard. Conflict is often triggered by a seemingly trivial incident. The incident itself is usually of little importance, since fights are rarely focused on a single issue. Instead they are spontaneous responses to tension and to real or imagined grievances which have built up over a period of time. Fights are invariably associated with excessive drinking and not surprisingly occur most often on Thursday and Friday evenings—the days of heaviest alcohol consumption, following receipt of the dole. These facets of Traveller society have parallels among some American Indians. Garabino, writing about urban Indians, suggests that excessive drinking and belligerence among men are directly linked to their emasculated status.

> The strain and guilt feelings of failure to play the role of head of the family may produce an increased tendency to turn to alcohol

as escape. Frequently physical conflict between the man and woman increases, that is, wife beatings increase (1971:186).

Marital fights among Tinkers are characterized by a great deal of commotion—screaming, yelling, breaking of windows, and throwing of dishes. Between the occasional volleys of punches is a continuous stream of name calling. The most serious denunciations are sexual: "whore," "bastard," and "cross-born bastard" (a bastard who does not know the identity of his father because his mother had relations with more than one man). The reputation of a husband's mother is attacked only at the height of a wife's anger. When one woman called her mother-in-law a "whore who slept with ten men," her husband rushed to a nearby scrap pile and picked up an iron bar. He threateningly demanded, "Honor my mother. Honor my mother or I'll knock your fuckin' head off." It is not uncommon for other families in camp to gather silently and watch; in fact, women often encourage bystanders because the presence of others may restrain their husbands. Unless there is real danger of serious injury, however, onlookers rarely intervene.

Fighting often relieves the tension between spouses. The morning after a fight, husbands and wives frequently are on friendly terms again, and the conflict of the night before is blamed on "the drink." (Again, the role of drinking as a sanctioned "time out" and as a recognized excuse for antagonistic behavior is apparent.) But without resolution of the underlying problems, the cycle begins again. In some families conflict takes place on such a regular basis that its occurrence can almost be predicted (and often is). It should also be noted that some women, especially the older and more traditional, consider a beating a sign that their husbands still care about them. Liebow notes a similar pattern among lower-class ghetto families in which the husband is unemployed. A beating offered women "some tangible evidence that her husband cared about her, about them as a family, and that he was willing to fight to protect his (nominal) status as head of the family" (Liebow 1967:135). Holylanders gossiped about one family in which the husband cared so little about his wife that he "never laid a hand on her."

Mother-Son Ties. Another factor contributing to marital strain is the strong emotional tie Tinker men maintain with their mothers long after they have established families of their own. The bond between mothers and sons is based on the patrilineal bias of Traveller society. A young woman living in the camp of her husband's kin group is often treated as an outsider by her mother-in-law and denied expressions of support by her husband's kin. In this setting, young wives rely heavily on the children they bear for affective satisfaction. Through the years especially strong ties of sentiment develop between mothers and sons, and it is not surprising that Traveller mothers come to regard their sons' wives as invaders of their affective world.[4]

Often a wife may find herself in competition with her mother-in-law for her husband's affection and devotion. Upon returning from the pub in the evening, the middle-aged Brien sons regularly stopped first at their mother's hut for a chat before going home to their own wives. The following remark made by Tom Brien reveals the feelings of many men: "I love me wife a lot. But to tell the truth, I love me mother more."

Mothers are very possessive of their sons and easily become jealous if they feel they have not received enough attention. Jealousy sometimes prompts them to create trouble between their sons and their wives. In an attempt to assert authority over her daughters-in-law, seventy-year-old Winnie occasionally insisted on serving her sons dinner even though their wives were already preparing a meal. In at least one instance, Winnie was responsible for a son beating his wife when she intimated that the woman had been seeing another man in camp.

Conflict between women and their mothers-in-law and the related marital strains have increased in the city, where large camps and increased sedentarism permit a greater degree of patrilocality (residence in the camp of the husband's kin group). In the past, the small size of travel groups resulted in many married sons living

---

[4]Strong mother-son ties have also been noted among the Irish peasantry (Arensberg and Kimball 1940) and the Irish working class (Humphreys 1966).

apart from their parents, at least for part of the year. But in urban areas there is virtually no restriction on the number of married couples who can adopt patrilocal residence. As women become more assertive, however, they sometimes refuse to live with their husband's kin group. One of Winnie's sons, at his wife's insistence, lives two miles from Holylands; and another daughter-in-law agreed to live in the camp only on the condition that her husband park their wagon at the opposite end of the field from his mother.

Separation as an Adaptive Response. One response to the instability of marriage relationships has been temporary separation. Separation, which usually involves the wife leaving her husband, is a safety-valve preventing a permanent breach of the marriage bond. When relations between a husband and wife become intolerably tense or hostile, the woman leaves. In effect, desertion by Tinker women represents the same response to conflict that shifting does for the entire family. It is a short-range solution to problems inherent in modern Traveller marriages.

Separation is greatly facilitated in Dublin, where the large population of Tinkers makes it likely that women will have close kin living nearby. Although desertion was not unknown in the past, it was considerably more difficult, since few wives would have known the exact location of their kin at any one time and most had no means of transportation.

Most spouses, after a much-needed respite from married life, soon become lonely for one another and seek to reunite. The length of separations vary from a few days to several months, depending upon the seriousness of the marriage breakdown, the eagerness of the spouses to get back together, and the distance the wife travels in deserting. Occasionally a woman may go as far as England in order to join relatives, in which case she is not likely to rush back because of the cost of the trip. Most women go to the residence of their natal family or, in the case of older women whose parents are deceased, to the camp of a married brother or sister. Once there, women usually enjoy the chance to visit kinsmen and escape domestic responsibilities for a while.

When women desert they often leave some of their children behind in their husbands' care. This is a form of punishment, since child-care responsibilities are a considerable burden on

Traveller men. It is also a form of insurance, because it results in a greater eagerness on the part of men to achieve reconciliation.

Men usually act as though they are glad to be free of their wives and deny any intention of retrieving them. To admit loneliness or despair would be a sign of weakness. If a wife stays away too long, however, she shows disdain for her husband, and the man's prestige may suffer. Within a few weeks most husbands seek the assistance of their parents or a brother in recovering their wives. Less fequently, the woman returns of her own volition.

Changing Courtship and Marriage Patterns

Before examining the changes which have occurred in Traveller courtship and marriage, it is necessary to describe briefly the traditional patterns. In the past, courtship was rare. The activities of teenage girls were sharply circumscribed: they were not allowed to mix with, much less date, members of the opposite sex (MacRitchie 1889; MacGreine 1931). In the words of one mother:

> Travellin' girls was not allowed to see no boys. If they seen boys down the road they daren't pull up, they'd have to pass right on. They couldn't talk to no boy and they couldn't make no weddin' of their own (Maggie McDonagh, age 49).

Parents feared that courtship would lead to premarital sex, which could ruin their daughter's reputation and damage the family's as well. Travellers placed a high value on chastity. Girls were expected to be virgins at marriage, and if there was any doubt the groom's parents could call a "provin' match" in which the prospective bride had to swear on the Bible before a priest that she had never had sexual relations.

Parents kept a close watch on their daughters.

> Their mothers was always with them. Always watchin' and not lettin' them go nowhere. A good mother kept her daughters under her skirt (Nan Driscoll, age 56).

Close supervision was possible in the rural setting because camps were small and isolated from nearby villages as well as from other Travellers. Parents would leave the group if they knew that their daughter was interested in a boy in camp.

By custom, marriages were arranged by the parents. Known as "matches," they were usually drawn between families who travelled the same territory; they were generally contracted in the spring or summer at county fairs. Often the boy and girl did not know one another. Individuals known as "matchmakers" were sometimes relied upon to locate suitable mates and to arrange meetings of the parents. Before the actual marriage ceremony, the bride and groom were introduced; their desires were considered but not necessarily heeded. Usually within several days of a match being "drawn," the marriage ceremony was performed.

Until the early 1900s, marriage in the Church or by legal civil ceremony does not appear to have been common. The exact nature of the ceremony Travellers followed, however, is unclear. According to MacRitchie:

> The only necessary marriage ceremony needed by the tinkers generally is for the man and woman to jump together hand and hand, over the 'budget'—as the box containing the materials used by the tinsman is called (1889:351).

Various other rites have been mentioned in the literature, including the bride and groom clasping hands over the back of a donkey while reciting a benediction. But it is difficult to know how reliable these stories are, since Tinkers have spun tales about other exotic customs which had little or no basis in fact. As Rehfisch (1961) speculates about Scottish Tinkers, it is not improbable that such ceremonies as "jumping the budget" may have been carried out in front of villagers in the hope of collecting money. Considering the minimum of ritual surrounding other rites of passage and the failure of Travellers to recall any specific ceremony, it seems likely that little protocol was attached to marriage. Most likely, having sexual relations was more important to consummating the union than ceremony.

Today, nearly all Tinkers are married in the Church. The introduction of State welfare benefits has been a stimulant for all Travellers to obtain a legal marriage, since without a marriage certificate a man cannot claim his wife and children as dependents.

Although the majority of Tinker marriages today are still arranged by the parents, an increasing number of young people are selecting their own mates. This is clearly the result of the increased contact and dating among adolescents that has occurred in urban areas. Parents' attitudes toward courtship and the value they place on premarital chastity have changed little, but their ability to supervise their adolescent children has. In camps such as Holylands there may be a dozen or more unattached teenagers. In this setting, where boys and girls come into frequent contact, dating is inevitable despite parental restrictions. At Holylands, teenagers leaving camp in their respective peer groups meet later in nearby cinemas or shops. There are also many opportunities for undetected meetings within camp and in the surrounding fields and thickets at night. Parents now recognize that sexual promiscuity is increasing; social workers report an increasing, although still small, number of illegitimate pregnancies.

The influence of movies, which Tinker youths attend regularly, and contact with settled adolescents through begging and scavenging are also important. In both contexts itinerant youths assimilate modern ideas of courtship and romance. Aware of their own "backwardness," they are often quick to imitate what they observe in mainstream Irish society.

One method parents have of coping with adolescent dating and courtship is to move from the area. During the period of fieldwork, several families left Holylands when they suspected their daughters were dating. A major factor in Davy Joyce's decision to shift his family was finding a charm bracelet that a boy in camp had given his thirteen-year-old daughter. But many parents are beginning to recognize that changing residence is only a temporary solution at best. For as long as the family remains in the city, there is little hope of eliminating illicit courtships.

When a courting couple wishes to marry, they may seek the permission of their parents. But when it is known in advance that the parents will object, usually because of the prospective spouse's family background or because another match has been planned, the couple may elope or make a "run-away match." Merely by staying away together one or more nights, the pair may force their parents into permitting them to marry, since it is then assumed that the girl has lost her virginity. Tom and Ali had been seeing one another for about a month when they decided to marry. When Tom's brother approached Ali's parents with the proposal, however, he was flatly refused. Her parents objected on the grounds that Tom's family were drunkards, often in trouble with the police. Several days later Ali failed to return from begging and let it be known that she was "sleeping out" with Tom. After a violent family argument in which he beat his wife for failing to keep the girl under control, Ali's father went to Tom's family and made arrangements for the wedding.

Early Marriage as an Adaptive Response. Many parents have responded to the weakening of their control over adolescent sons and daughters by arranging matches for them at an increasingly early age.

> Years ago the girls would be eighteen before they was married, but now they're gettin' married at fourteen and fifteen. I think the parents do be glad to get rid of them. The little girls is goin' out of control, against their mothers and fathers. They're off to the pictures and meeting up with boys. The parents is glad to get them married young. Then they're off the parents' hands, and they can't give them no scandal (Maggie McDonagh, age 49).

In this way, girls may be married before they have had a chance to become sexually involved with boys. Moreover, adolescents without much prior contact with the opposite sex are less likely to object to a match proposed by the parents. Never having dated, they do not have strong mate preferences of their own.

Early matched marriages are also an attempt by parents to cope with the increasing delinquency of adolescent boys and, to a lesser degree, girls. With few chores and no recreational outlets, Traveller youths roam about the camp and city finding mischievous activities with which to pass the time. Boys are often involved in shoplifting and petty theft and have been responsible for a good deal of vandalism, much of it to facilities in their own camps. A few have become involved in more serious crimes, such as breaking and entering and larceny. A similar increase in adolescent anti-social behavior has been noted among Eskimos, who like Tinkers previously lived in small, dispersed bands but have recently moved into large settlements (Graburn 1969). As Graburn notes, this

Plate 16. Teenage marriage among Holylands families, Dublin. (*Photo by Pat Langan*)

behavior results not only from the increase in population size but also from an increase in opportunities for adolescents to be away from their parents' supervision.

By arranging earlier matches for their children, parents hope that the responsibilities of family life will keep them out of trouble. The fact that adolescents over age sixteen do not qualify as dependents for the purpose of State welfare benefits and do not receive their own benefits until age eighteen also contributes to the parents' desire to have them marry.

The trend toward earlier matched marriages is confirmed by the results of a demographic survey (see Table 3). Traveller males and females now marry approximately three and two years earlier respectively than Travellers in the previous generation. Moreover, some girls (13 of the 37 recorded in Table 3) are being married at ages fourteen and fifteen. This decline in marital age is not restricted to Dublin, but there is no question that the change has been most dramatic there.

The sharp increase in early teenage marriages has prompted the Dublin Itinerant Settlement Committee to seek the cooperation

Table 3. Mean Age at Marriage Among the Tinker Population[5]

Sex of Traveller	Mean Age of 37 Traveller Marriages in Dublin (1969-73)	Mean Age of 40 Traveller Marriages in Rural Areas (persons born prior to 1930)
Male	20.0	23.6
Female	17.2	19.3

Source: Statistics on Dublin Traveller marriages were obtained from the author's demographic survey and were updated by records provided by ISC social workers. Statistics in the second column were obtained from an earlier demographic survey (Crawford and Gmelch 1974) and from the Commission Report (R.C.I. 1963:124).

of the clergy in establishing procedures to stop or at least postpone "juvenile marriages." In 1972, the Archbishop of Dublin appointed a priest to handle this matter. Now all couples under age twenty wishing to marry must first apply to the appointed priest and then wait a minimum of three months and go through marriage counseling before being granted permission to marry. The ISC and the clergy hope that many prospective marriages— which are normally matched one week and carried out the next— will dissolve before the three months have elapsed. And if not, the couple will at least have had the benefit of marriage instruction.

The new regulations have been an outrage to some families who insist on their right to marry their children whenever they wish. Some have travelled to the countryside in the hope of finding a priest who is either unaware of or opposed to the new procedures and who will perform the ceremony. Nonetheless, by 1975 the new regulations did appear to be having some effect in slowing down the trend toward early marriage.

Close-kin Marriage as an Adaptive Response. There has been a marked increase in the number of first- and second-cousin

[5] In comparison with these figures, the average age of grooms in the settled Irish population in 1969 was 28.1, while the average age of brides in 1969 was 25.3 years (S.A. 1974:15).

marriages among urban Travellers. Of thirty-seven marriages recorded in Dublin between 1969 and 1973, twelve were between first cousins and four involved second cousins.[6] Others were between an uncle and niece, an aunt and nephew, and a forty-two-year-old widower and his fourteen-year-old daughter. With one obvious exception, all of these marriages were arranged by the parents. In the past, unions between first cousins were uncommon, except among a few families in the West. As Mary Maughm recalls:

> Years ago you wouldn't hear tell of it. It was a scandalous way of goin' on, and you'd nearly be put in the newspapers. Everybody'd be talkin', sayin' you couldn't get no other body so you married your cousin.

Yet in the past five years Mary herself has matched two of her sons with her brother's daughters.

The increase in close-kin marriages can be viewed as a response to the uncertain and ambivalent relations which exist among different kin groups in urban areas. As previously mentioned, Travellers in the past drew mates from other lineages

Table 4. Kin Relationship of Couples Married in Dublin (1969-1973)

Relationship of Bride and Groom	Marriages not Arranged by Parents	Marriages Arranged by Parents
No relationship	11	6
First Cousins	0	12
Second Cousins	0	4
Other	1	3
Total	12	25

Source: Author's survey and records of ISC social workers.

---

[6]In the provincial town of Mullingar, which has had a large Tinker population since the early 1950s, half of sixty-one married couples questioned were either first or second cousins (records of Dr. M.P. Flynn, 1975).

travelling the same territory. Since urbanization, traditional marriage alliance groups have often become widely dispersed or are no longer in regular contact with one another. And parents are reluctant to make matches for their children with lineages they do not already have established ties with, especially those from other parts of the country. In the words of one informant:

> You've got Travellers from all parts of Ireland mixing up here
> [in Dublin]. Those from the East don't know the background of
> the people belonging to the West, some of them do be very rough.
> And those from the West don't know them from the East. Travel-
> lin' People are afeard to get in with strangers. But if you marry a
> cousin you know what you're getting into (Mick Driscoll, age 60).

In this setting where there is great uncertainty and often hostility toward other kin groups, close-kin marriages are viewed as a means of strengthening the local kin group. Parents are then secure that, should fighting break out with another group, as it sometimes does, their married sons and daughters will be close by to lend support. Rehfisch (1961) notes that among Scottish Tinkers, who are more acculturated to mainstream society, close-kin marriages declined as families came to rely more on the police and the State legal system to provide protection.

The preference for drawing matches with close kin is also a response to the instability of marital relationships. To some extent, close-kin marriages insure that spouses remain together. In case of conflict, the wife's relatives can more easily intervene on her behalf if they are also related to the husband. And when a wife deserts her husband there is much less difficulty in reuniting the couple because both sets of relatives are related. As one man explained:

> If the wife runs off, the boy has no trouble gettin' her back be-
> cause she's goin' to go back to her family. And her family is the
> boy's aunt and uncle. They're all the one people. They're all the
> one blood. But if you marry a stranger, if she's gone, well that's
> it . . . she could be gone (Mick Driscoll, age 60).

The following incident is illustrative. Paddy and Nan are first cousins; their fathers are brothers. They had been married less than a year when Nan left Paddy and returned to her parents' camp in Carlow, fifty miles from Dublin. She had left him on several earlier occasions but travelled only as far as the camp of other relatives in the Dublin area, and she had always returned within a few weeks. This separation, however, was more serious. In the fight preceding it she had broken all the windows in their trailer as well as their dishes and stormed out of Holylands vowing never to return. A month passed with no sign that she was ready to reconsider. Paddy finally asked his father, a cousin, and myself to accompany him to Carlow to attempt a reconciliation. Once there, Paddy went to the pub while his relatives discussed the situation and pressured Nan to return with her husband. After much crying and grief she agreed to return "for the sake of relations" between the two families.

Thus in close-kin marriages there are built-in social controls in the form of cooperation between the two kin groups which help prevent marriage breakdowns. Both sets of parents have an interest in seeing that the union lasts, since such matches are made at least partially to cement ties between the families themselves. The resolution of marital conflict is more problematic when there is no existing pattern of cooperation between the two sets of relatives. In fact, intervention of the wife's kin into the affairs of the patrilocally-based couple would not be tolerated.

Tinkers also express the belief that marriages between cousins are naturally stronger unions than others. According to one informant:

> Travellin' People believe that cousins will have more nature for one another, and they won't use no violence on each other. The boy won't kick up the woman so bad if she is his cousin. If they aren't happy together, they may stick on just for the sake of bein' so near a relation, bein' of the same blood (Katie Flynn, age 32).

For the most part, the Church and the Dublin ISC appear less concerned with the degree of consanguinity of the marrying pair than their age. Travellers have had little difficulty in securing Church dispensations despite the prohibition in Canon Law against marriages within the third degree of kindred. Many priests apparently feel that the possibility of the couple living together unwed would be a "greater evil" than permitting first or second cousins to marry. Obtaining a proper dispensation is especially important to some Travellers who believe that without it there are no safe-guards against possible ill effects of inbreeding. They believe that through some divine power, the Church's dispensation actually changes or "cleans" the blood of the parents. Some Holylanders attributed the two deaf-and-dumb children in one family to the fact that the parents, who are first cousins, had married without a dispensation.

CHAPTER SEVEN

Settlement

In the preceding three chapters we have examined the economic and social adaptation of Tinkers living in urban camps and sites. This chapter will look at the increasing number of families who have been housed in the settled community. At the time of the 1974 census, 468 families or 27 percent of Ireland's itinerant population were living in houses—largely through the efforts of the nationwide, volunteer Itinerant Settlement Movement. The adjustment to settled life is not easy, and many families have returned to the road. This chapter focuses on the reasons Travellers' settle and the difficulties they often encounter in adapting to life in the settled community—not just in Dublin but in all urban areas where itinerants have been housed. The settlement patterns and housing policies of two towns in which Tinkers have made a highly successful adjustment are also examined.

Background

Prior to the current Settlement Movement, the only instance in which a sizeable number of Travellers were housed occurred in the 1930s. Then, the newly independent Irish State initiated a widespread building program aimed at eradicating the shacks and dilapidated dwellings common in many Irish towns and cities. As a result of the Housing Act of 1931, an estimated one hundred Traveller families who had been squatting in slum areas (primarily during the winter) were placed in public housing among sedentary folk. In some towns, such as Tralee (County Kerry), Granard (County Longford), and Athlone (County Westmeath), an entire terrace (row) of up to thirty houses was allocated to Tinkers. This program was not designed specifically to aid Travellers; rather it was to provide better accommodation for all families occupying substandard dwellings in town.

The history of this early housing experiment is sketchy. It is clear, however, that many of the Traveller families who were housed eventually returned to the road. Of the thirty-one tenants originally settled in St. Mel's Terrace in Athlone in 1934, only five remain today. In many cases the families who left were replaced by other Tinkers who lived there for a time and then returned to the road themselves. Judging from the names listed in the records of the town clerk, approximately sixty different Tinker families have resided in St. Mel's since 1934. Twenty-six of these families, however, transferred to other public housing estates in Athlone where, away from the ghetto conditions of the former terrace and among settled people, many eventually assimilated.[1]

In general, families who remained in the original terraces have not integrated. Most still identify themselves as Travellers and maintain ties with the road; often their children marry into families that are still nomadic. The stigma attached to being housed in these neighborhoods is so strong that even families from settled backgrounds who live there may be identified as Tinkers and treated accordingly by local people. One such individual complained that his children were taunted by school classmates and that they had difficulty obtaining part-time jobs solely because of their residence in St. Mel's. "It's no differ how respectable you are, as long as you live in Mel's they class you a Tinker."

Between the 1930s and the start of the present Settlement Movement, there were no direct attempts to offer housing to itinerants. Some towns in the West of Ireland did house a small number of families during the mid-1950s, when the high rate of outmigration from the area created numerous vacancies in public housing. But the discriminatory practices of most local authorities undoubtedly prevented other families who wanted to settle

---

[1]Personal communication of Michael Flynn, Westmeath County Medical Officer.

from being housed. Housing applications from Tinkers were routinely passed over in favor of settled folk. Mick and Nan Driscoll were on a housing list in one Midlands town for seven years until they finally left in frustration and migrated to Dublin. Each time Mick had inquired about a house he was told that his name was near the top of the list and that he need not come back until contacted. Considering the criteria used by local authorities to assess housing need and determine priority (condition of the family's present dwelling, extent of overcrowding, family size, and illness in the family), most Travellers should have been given top preference.

The force behind the current effort to provide Tinkers the opportunity to settle are the seventy local ISCs. These committies and their National coordinating committee in Dublin—The Irish Council for Travelling People— have pressured the State and local governments into providing houses as well as sites for Travellers. Initially the Movement, with government support, concentrated its efforts on providing serviced campsites, believing Tinkers were unable to make the transition to housing directly from the road. In the words of one official:

> The first step towards ultimate integration of itinerants is the provision by local authorities of serviced camping sites. Such sites provide the necessary springboard for the itinerants. . . . They give local voluntary groups a working area where they can give the itinerants advice and help them to map out a settled way of life. These sites then act as a bridge between the itinerants and the settled community and help both communities towards a mutual understanding. (*Irish Times,* Dec. 15, 1969)

A number of smaller towns, acting primarily on the conviction that settling Travellers on sites was only postponing their integration into mainstream society, began lobbying for houses. The successful adjustment families made in these areas has in turn caused other committees to rethink their policies. There has also been a growing realization within the Movement that no single policy will meet the needs and desires of all Tinkers. Consequently, many ISCs are now trying to offer various modes of settlement: "halts" with minimal services for transient families, "sites" with chalets for families who desire amenities and accommodation but wish to pursue itinerant occupations and remain among their own group, and housing for families who desire permanent settlement and, in some cases, integration. One result of the shift away from the dogmatic position that sites are the only solution to settlement has been a dramatic increase in the number of families being housed.

Because of the housing shortage in large urban areas—Dublin, Cork, and Limerick—proportionately fewer itinerants have been settled there than in provincial towns. Only forty families or about 10 percent of Dublin's Tinker population have been housed, compared with 50 percent or more in many provincial towns.

As a rule, Tinkers have been housed in lower working-class neighborhoods. And with one exception to be discussed later, all have been placed in public housing. Most are duplex-type dwellings containing two or three small bedrooms, a combined kitchen-living room, and a bathroom. Weekly rents are based on the family's income; since nearly all Travellers are on the dole, it is minimal, rarely more than two pounds per week.

Settled Irish have strongly opposed the housing of Tinkers in their communities. Upon learning of ISC or local authority plans to house Travellers in their neighborhoods, residents have often organized protest marches, circulated petitions, and in some cases picketed County Council offices and threatened rent strikes. In several instances settled folk have moved out of the neighborhood (usually by securing a transfer to another public housing estate) in protest. Local authorities have often found it difficult to fill vacancies in houses adjacent to Tinker families. Opposition to the provision of sites has been equally strong. The most frequently voiced fears are of three main types: (1) fear of disruption to the neighborhood caused by begging, drinking, and general rowdyism; (2) fear of criminal acts, including trespass, theft, and vandalism; and (3) fear that the status or reputation of the neighborhood will suffer. Private homeowners are also concerned that property values will decline. And in the case of sites, there is the additional fear of hazards to public health.

In most cases, protests have pitted local residents and residents' associations against ISCs and local authorities; generally, Travellers have not been directly involved. In one widely publicized incident in 1970, neighboring residents physically attempted to prevent a Tinker widow and her two children from entering the house they had been allocated by the local authority. This action was taken despite the fact that the family had been on Galway City's housing list for ten years and for the previous two years had been living in wretched conditions in a derelict house without gas, water, or electricity. Yet 80 percent of the local residents signed a letter of protest. And when the housing authority refused to yield to their demands, they smashed windows and boarded up the doors to the house. On the day the family arrived to establish tenancy, an angry throng of approximately three hundred of their prospective neighbors blocked the path to the house and taunted them with placards and shouts of "No Tinkers here" and "We want our own people housed." Only through the aid of local police was the family able to move in.[2] Today they are accepted by their neighbors and are friends with some.

In another incident, Paddy McDonagh purchased a house in Moate, a small town in the Midlands, with the help of the County Medical Officer. Two days before he and his family were to move in, several local residents set fire to the structure, destroying the upstairs and roof. Paddy hired a carpenter to make repairs, but local residents prevented him from working. The McDonaghs then gave up and moved to Dublin, to Holylands.

Motivative Factors in Settlement

What are the incentives to settle? Why have so many itinerant families left the road to take housing? The decision to settle is a reaction to what are perceived as unfavorable existing conditions of itinerant life, contrasted with projections regarding the rewards of living in a house. The benefits of housing must outweigh the Travellers' attachment to the predictable and familiar environment of the road. The perceived rewards must also be strong enough to overcome their fears and insecurities about living among settled folk.

---

[2] See the *Irish Times*, September 6-10, 1970, for a complete account.

Travelling life has become increasingly difficult for many families in recent years. Finding a good campsite is now troublesome, as many locations have been purposefully fenced off or barricaded. Some towns have passed by-laws prohibiting camping within a certain radius of the town. This is particularly true of communities that have settled a number of Tinker families; they feel they have done their "fair share" and that additional Travellers should be some other town's responsibility. Increased traffic on most roads has diminished the pleasures of travel by horse and cart and has made it more dangerous. In view of these factors, coupled with the loss of their former trades, Tinkers often say, "there's nothin' left on the road."

The difficulties in pursuing a nomadic way of life explain why many Travellers are opting for settlement, but they reveal little about why families move into houses as opposed to official campsites. One reason is the amenities available in houses which are not present on the road or in many sites: electricity—and hence the possibility of television—hot running water and baths, and gas for cooking and heating. Such benefits are especially desirable in the winter, when life on the road is hardest. Tinker women desire housing more then men, no doubt because their daily tasks of cooking, washing, and child care are made easier by the presence of such conveniences. The importance of amenities as an inducement to settle is revealed by the fact that the Travellers' desire for conventional housing is less in areas where fully serviced sites exist. Few families living on Dublin's fully equipped sites, for example, accepted public housing when it was offered to them.

The decision to settle, however, involves more than just a consideration of amenities. Many Travellers view housing as a solution to or escape from the problems endemic to itinerant life. Many adults are discontent with their present circumstances—excessive drinking, conflict, jealousies, and strong levelling pressures. They believe that despite material improvements, the quality of life on the road has declined—that there are fewer satisfactions today. Unhappiness with itinerant life and the negative valuation many Travellers have of their own identity is sometimes transformed into the hope that their children will marry settled folk.

Housing is often seen by parents as a solution to problems in disciplining children. Parents in large urban camps find it especially difficult to control their children because the sheer size of the camp means that children are able to play beyond the reach of parental control. Remarking on the unruliness of her children, one mother who had previously been housed stated, "If I don't get me childer back into a house where I can keep a rein on 'em, they'll turn into pure savages." Young parents hope that if raised in a house, their children will receive a better education and will learn to mix with settled children and become "respectable." As Katie Flynn remarked:

> The childer that is reared on the road is wild. They don't go with manners. The childer has to be raised in a house if they're ever goin' to be fit for settlin' down and livin' like respectable people.

When asked why they moved into a house, parents often respond, "It's for the sake of the childer."

Being a house-dweller also confers a certain amount of prestige. A house is more than just a physical structure; it is a symbol of status, achievement, and, to some extent, social acceptance. It has a dramatic effect on the way in which the family perceives itself and is perceived by others (Schoor 1970). In social contexts in which housed families are anonymous (that is, where their background is unknown), they may use their status as householders as a denial of their Tinker identity. On one occasion, for example, I met an individual whom I knew from other sources to be a housed Traveller. But when I engaged the man in conversation and asked him a question about Travellers, he responded, "I wouldn't know about that, sir. I'm not a Traveller. I live in a house."

The desire to pass as settled is not, however, the most important consideration of Travellers who take housing. Most Irish communities are too intimate and the populace too sensitive to the symbols of Tinker identity—appearance, accent, type of lorry or cart, surname, and so forth—for the family to conceal its itinerant background. This is sometimes achieved in Dublin but rarely outside. If the motive for settlement is to escape one's identity as a Tinker, that is best achieved in England. There the English, and especially the Pakistani, West Indian, and other emigrant residents of the slum neighborhoods in which some Travellers have settled, are insensitive to the cues that signal Tinker identity.

Thus Travellers living in flats or houses are often able to pass as poor, working-class Irish.

Finally, it should be noted that in some towns families have moved into houses largely because the alternative form of settlement—official sites—does not exist. Families who wish to settle in these areas have no choice but to accept housing.

The families who most desire housing tend to be in the middle range in terms of income and status. In contrast, the well-off families pursue occupations such as large-scale scrap dealing, asphalt laying, and roadside trading, which often require mobility. More importantly, these families are comfortable in their present circumstances: many own two trailers and are well equipped with bottled-gas stoves and lamps, battery-operated television sets, and other conveniences. This segment of the Tinker population closely resembles the wealthier English Gypsies who want no part of settled life, seeing it as both a loss of freedom and a hindrance to their occupations and source of livelihood. At the other extreme are the down-and-out or "rough" itinerant families, who because of alcoholism cannot manage the expenses involved in living in a house.

In general, interest in housing is greatest in the West of Ireland, where scavenging and begging are least remunerative. Moreover, the cultural gap between Tinkers and settled Irish is often smaller in the West, where many people have only recently emerged from a peasant background. Overall, housed Tinkers seemed to feel more comfortable with their neighbors in Western towns than they do in the more modern East. In a questionnaire survey in which ISC chairpersons were asked what percentage of families in their districts desired housing, it was reported that more than 85 percent of the Travellers in eight western counties wanted to be housed. In contrast, the Committees in five prosperous eastern counties reported that only half their families desired settlement. In both cases the figures are probably inflated: committees tend to overestimate the number of families desiring settlement, both because it helps gain public support for their policies and because many volunteers sincerely fail to understand why Tinkers would not want to be housed.

Adaptation to Housing

The situations in which Travellers have adapted most successfully to housing will be discussed in the next section. Here our concern is with the difficulties Travellers commonly encounter in housing, which often result in families returning to the road.

Families taking a house for the first time are customarily unprepared for the expenses—rent and electricity, gas, and water bills—since on the road virtually everything is free. These expenses reduce the amount of cash they have to spend on their own leisure activities. Like most poverty groups accustomed to a day-to-day existence, Tinkers tend to be present-time-oriented relative to the middle classes who plan and save, viewing the future as a progression upward to better positions and higher statuses. Hence Travellers find it difficult to postpone immediate gratifications for future concerns. Mylee and Mary Driscoll were allocated a house in a Dublin suburb. After the first two months, during which time the bills went unpaid, Mary learned how much money would have to be put aside each week. She then attempted to hide the money so there would be less temptation to spend it. Nevertheless, over the next four months they continued to fall behind in their payments, because neither one was able to ignore the savings. Whenever bored or frustrated, they removed some of the money and went to the pub, always promising each other to repay the loan but never able to. Finally, threatened with eviction, they left the house and put up a tent at Holylands.

Housing can make the pursuit of Traveller occupations difficult. Neighbors object to the unsightliness of large scrap piles, and frequently there is just no room for storing scrap in public housing schemes. This is especially true in the cities where the high population density and small yards make it virtually impossible to stockpile scrap metal at one's residence. Keeping horses in public housing is equally problematic, though it is sometimes done. Most local authorities prohibit the ownership of animals other than dogs and cats. And although families housed in smaller provincial towns are often able to arrange livery with nearby farmers, in the cities this is more difficult. Once housed, many women feel compelled to cease begging in the desire to be accepted by their settled neighbors. Some travel to other towns or across the city to beg where they will not be recognized. Hence housing not only requires additional expenses but may also mean a reduction in real income.

The attitudes of the local settled community also affect the adjustment Travellers make to housing. When Travellers are shunned, the temptation to return to the road and rejoin their social equals is great. This is especially true when a family is housed alone, without the reinforcement and security of having close kinsmen nearby.

Although in some ways unique, the following example illustrates the importance Tinkers may place on acceptance by their settled neighbors. Red Ned and Margaret were allocated a house in Ballyfermot, a working-class neighborhood in Dublin. Being "respectable" Travellers and unknown to local residents, they hoped to conceal their itinerant background and pass as ordinary country people. Before taking occupancy, Red Ned bought each member of the family a new set of clothes. Once in the house he attempted to plant flowers in the front yard. However, since he had never gardened before and dared not admit his ignorance to his neighbors, his attempt failed. Margaret did not beg in the area, although she occasionally took the bus across the city to visit her former patronesses. They kept their new address a secret from all but a few relatives to prevent visitors and their unmistakable "Traveller" lorries and green Escort vans from revealing their identity. After they were housed for about three months, a settlement committee worker related their success to a Dublin journalist. The news story not only revealed that Red Ned and Margaret were Tinkers but also included a picture taken of the family along their tent a year earlier. Without waiting to see how their neighbors would respond, they moved back onto the road.

Other factors also contributed to their decision to abandon the house. Lonely for the companionship of his relatives, Red Ned was spending a great deal of his time away from the house visiting. This created some conflict between him and Margaret. And the fear that sooner or later a slip of the tongue would reveal their real identity to their neighbors was an ever-present anxiety. Even though their immediate neighbors had been friendly, Red Ned and Margaret always felt out of place.

As mentioned above, a sense of isolation and loneliness often develops when families are housed apart from their kinsmen.

Travellers are highly gregarious, like most people raised in impoverished and crowded conditions (cf. Schoor 1970), and they greatly desire the companionship of others. Most of their forms of entertainment, such as drinking, gambling, and story-telling, involve or require a group. The isolation and loneliness housed Tinkers feel is often compounded by their inability to relate to their settled neighbors. As one informant lamented:

> I can't talk to these people [settled neighbors]. They talk about things I don't know nothin' about. The things I can talk about they wouldn't be interested in. I can pass the whole day talkin' with another Travellin' man, but I can't say nothin' to these here (John McCarthy, age 45).

If, on the other hand, too many kinsmen live nearby, problems of another kind may develop. Frequently the residence of the housed family becomes a gathering place for Tinkers to drink, watch television, and escape the damp and cold in winter. The drunkenness and noise that sometimes result may alienate neighbors and erode whatever support the housed family may have in the community. Tom and Mary Delaney had been settled for almost six months and their children enrolled in the local school. Then relatives shifted back into the area and made camp down the road. The Delaneys' kinsmen began visiting the house to get water, use the bath, and the like. Then, during a drinking binge one evening, a fight broke out during which several windows of an adjacent house as well as the windshield of a neighbor's car were broken. The next day the Delaneys left the house. Several months later Tom Delaney remarked, "If I ever get another house I won't tell a soul [the address], not even me mother." Such incidents are sometimes intentional, provoked by relatives who are jealous of the housed family's enhanced status and who feel threatened by the possibility of their cutting off or minimizing their ties with the road. Again we see the presence of levelling mechanisms.

As previously discussed, Tinkers cope with many of their problems by physically moving away from them. Even though some families wish to remain settled, shifting is often the only solution they know to certain problems. Few families are able to remain settled, following the death of a member of the household. In the past, Travellers abandoned or destroyed the wagon of the deceased and left the area. After being housed continuously for more than five years, one family left their home and returned to the road following the death of one of their eight children.

Illness is sometimes blamed on conditions related to living in a house and may be cause for a family returning to the road. Tinkers often complain that the heat and the air in houses are unhealthy. Some leave doors and windows open for ventilation. Recently two families turned down housing in a new Dublin estate because the homes were centrally heated and lacked fireplaces.

Another difficulty Tinkers encounter in adjusting to settled life is boredom. This is especially true for men, who have lost many of their former pastimes and have few new activities to fill the void. And because of restrictions placed on scavenging and keeping horses, they have even more idle time than those living on sites. Tom Brien, frustrated with his life in a house, had this to say:

> A person who was bred, born, and reared on the road is not going to be happy in a house. Travelling People need a lot of change, and a house to a Travelling man is like a prison. It keeps you in the one place all the time.

A few housed Travellers, like those settled on serviced sites, are able to satisfy their desire for change and travel by paying their rent in advance and abandoning their homes during the summer months. Even several families from St. Mel's Terrace who have been housed for an entire generation close their homes and move onto the road during the summer.

Two Studies in Adaptation

While most Travellers experience problems in adapting to housing, in some areas they have less difficulty than in others. To understand the factors that make for a successful adaptation, this section examines the settlement policies of two towns in which large numbers of Tinkers have been housed with little apparent difficulty. "Success" as used here is a relative term referring to the average length of home occupancy and the level of acceptance the housed families have attained in the settled community.

Tuam, County Galway. Tuam, population 5000, is a regional trade center in Western Ireland. Since the mid-1950s approximately forty Traveller families have camped in the vicinity of the town.

Nine of the families were housed, one each year, by the local
housing authority prior to the formation of a Settlement Committee.
This was largely the result of vacancies occurring in public housing, as Tuam suffered a high rate of out-migration in the 1950s
and early 1960s. By 1965, when housing was again in short
supply, the local authority had ceased housing Travellers. In
1968 a local ISC was organized in Tuam. Ignoring the National
Settlement Movement policy of settling Travellers first on sites,
the Tuam committee pressured the local authority to house the
remaining thirty-one families camped in the area. Aware of the
ghetto conditions that had developed when Travellers were housed
together, as in St. Mel's Terrace in Athlone, the Bullring in Tralee,
and other housing experiments of the 1930s, the ISC pursued a
policy of dispersing Travellers with no more than two families
housed on the same block. By 1975 seventeen families had been
housed in this way, including nearly all the members of three
local kin groups. Only four families left their homes and returned
to the road, and two of these have since been rehoused. Because
of Tuam's rural location, most backyards are large enough to
allow for the storage of scrap metal. And several families have
been housed in renovated farm houses on the outskirts of the
town, where they are able to keep horses. The few families
still unhoused are awaiting vacancies and are temporarily accom-
modated in ISC trailers on the roadside.

Considering the brief time that most Tinkers have been
housed in Tuam, they have adapted well and are beginning to be
accepted by the settled community. The general condition of
their homes is on a par with that of their neighbors, and their
grooming and appearance has improved considerably with the
availability of washing facilities. Traveller women have made a
conscious effort to blend in with the settled population by discarding traditional items of clothing such as hair ribbons, long
aprons, and shawls. One of the most revealing changes has been
the cessation of house begging, except of the patronness-client
type. (Street begging has never been common in small provincial
towns.) Housed Travellers have also joined a number of clubs and
have participated in some town activities. Traveller boys have
become stalwarts of the local boxing club, and many of the younger girls have joined Girl Guides. Some men participated in a card
tournament held in the town, while others have joined the local
credit union and attend resident association meetings. Attendance
at Mass has also been high.

Although adult Travellers often mix freely with their neighbors, few have as yet developed close friendships. And there has been no intermarriage, the ultimate sign of acceptance and integration. Many Tinker children, however, have made friends with settled children at the clubs and school, and it seems likely that some will eventually marry into settled society.

Mullingar, County Westmeath. Mullingar, population 11,000, is located 50 miles west of Dublin in the geographical region known as the Midlands. Mullingar has unquestionably achieved the most success in Ireland in housing Travellers, and it is now widely cited by advocates of direct housing as evidence that Tinkers can adjust to housing directly from the road. Largely through the efforts of the County Medical Officer, Mullingar has permanently housed forty of its fifty-four itinerant families in the past nineteen years. From the beginning, families were dispersed through the town; the largest concentration of Tinkers in any one neighborhood is seven, and each has settled neighbors on either side.

What is unique to Mullingar is not its settlement pattern but the fact that twenty-five of the families own their homes. This is unprecedented in Ireland. Beginning in 1956, the County Medical Officer blocked the issuance of demolition orders on houses he knew to be structurally sound. No objections were raised when Traveller families took posession of them.[3] From their own resources and in some cases with the help of a government grant for renovating substandard dwellings, the new occupants made the necessary repairs. Under the Repairs Grant Scheme, the owner received one-third the estimated cost from the central government and one-third from the local housing authority. If the Traveller did most of the work himself, the grants would usually cover the cost of the materials.

Subsequently, the government sanctioned the payment of grants covering 40 percent of the cost (up to a maximum of £500) of homes purchased by Travellers for their own use. With this grant and the help of a loan from the County Council, some Mullingar Travellers are now purchasing homes valued up to £2500.

---

[3]The County Council took court action against one such family in 1950. After examining the house, however, the District Justice decided in favor of the Traveller family, thus setting a legal precedent for the future.

Since 1956, only six families have left their homes. The standards of housekeeping have been exceptionally high, and many families have made substantial home improvements. When John Joyce purchased his house for £900, the walls were crumbling from excessive dampness and the electrical wiring was faulty. During the first year, with his own savings and an additional government grant, he laid new linoleum floors, hired an electrician to rewire the house, and replastered the walls. Over the next two years he added an additional room, painted the exterior, and paved a driveway into the backyard. This house which was originally condemned, now has a market value of approximately £2000.

Three families now live in a new middle-class County Council estate. All three were first housed in Mullingar more than ten years ago and moved up twice to better homes before being offered a house in the new estate. The same degree of upward mobility in housing is as yet rare among Travellers outside Mullingar.

The housed Travellers have begun to integrate into the settled community. Nearly 100 percent of the children of compulsory school age (five to sixteen years) are enrolled in school, and a dozen adults attend night literacy classes. One girl has completed her second year in a private boarding school; her parents are paying the fees. Many adolescents have joined local youth clubs and mix with the settled community at large local dances. There is also some informal social mixing with settled neighbors, although few close friendships have yet developed. While there has been no intermarriage, some dating has taken place. Families on the whole still restrict their close relationships to other Travellers in the town. Significantly, some women and adolescents of both sexes have obtained regular employment, primarily factory and domestic jobs. Eight young men have joined the army.

Discussion. In the case of Mullingar, home ownership has been a primary factor in the Tinkers' successful adaptation to housing. Given the marginal, nomadic existence they have always been forced to live, a home of their own which no one can force them out of represents security, independence, and status. Housed families in Mullingar exhibit a degree of pride in their homes that does not appear to exist among Travellers in public housing. Nearly all the families have invested considerable amounts of money and labor in making repairs and improvements. A number of families have paved portions of their yards and built small sheds for the storage of scrap metal; nine have constructed additional rooms.

Significantly, Mullingar Tinkers demonstrate an increasing trend toward conspicuous consumption—a "keep up with the Joneses" ethic that is much less evident among Travellers in public housing. As one woman commented:

> The Travellers here are all trying to best one another, to see who can have the best house. If one of 'em paves the yard, they all want to pave the yard (Mary Rattigan, age 40).

There is little incentive, of course, to make such improvements in public housing, where dwellings will always belong to the town. The well-kept appearance of the Travellers' homes has played a considerable role in convincing local people that they are fit for housing. Although there were vigorous protests to the housing of itinerants in Mullingar in earlier years, they have been muted in recent times. There is less legitimacy for protest when Travellers are purchasing their own homes.

Interestingly, the Government Commission on Itinerancy rejected in 1960 the suggestion that substandard dwellings be allocated to Travellers. It was felt that such dwellings would only create "new and greater problems."

> Singly or collectively, the deliberate provision of substandard dwellings for itinerants would stigmatize those persons as inferior beings and could only widen the gap already existing between them and the settled population (R.C.I. 1963:63).

Yet the success Mullingar Tinkers have had in adapting to settlement and the progress they have made toward integration into the settled community can largely be attributed to the beneficial effects of home ownership. When compared with the experience of Tinkers in public housing, the Mullingar experiment seems to indicate that enabling families to own their dwellings should be a primary goal of local authorities. As Turner (1970) notes of lower-income families in developing nations, what the poor desire most is secure land tenure, and only secondarily an adequate dwelling and utilities.

Other factors contributed to the success of Travellers in adapting to settlement in both Tuam and Mullingar. Of major significance is the dispersion of families over several neighborhoods. This pattern avoids the ghetto-like conditions of the settlements of the 1930s. At the same time, the presence of one or two other Tinker families in the area has prevented the sense of isolation that often occurs when a family is housed alone. Most families are in favor of dispersed housing, provided they have some relatives close by. When the idea of a segregated Traveller housing estate was suggested to Holylanders, they said it would never work—there would be drinking, fighting, and vandalism, and ultimately the project would end in ruin. Goulet (1971) has noted the same negative attitude among Spanish Gypsies when the idea of a Gypsy "homeland" was raised.

Where Travellers and settled folk live side by side, communication between the two groups is promoted. And as Shibutani (1970) and others have noted, negative stereotypes held by the majority group begin to break down as interaction and familiarity with minority-group members increases. Furthermore, in a setting in which Tinkers interact regularly with settled neighbors, they become more sensitive to behaving in ways which are acceptable to settled folk. Most Traveller women in Tuam and Mullingar, for example, have sharply curtailed their begging activities. Although they discreetly visit their ladies and a few women still beg outside of town, they refrain from begging near home where they might be seen by neighbors. In contrast, the women of St. Mel's Terrace and those from other Traveller enclaves do not feel the same constraints. Nor do families in these areas feel compelled to maintain their yards and homes. It is not uncommon to see broken windows merely boarded over rather than replaced.

The adjustment to housing was made easier in both Tuam and Mullingar by the fact that entire kin groups have been settled. This reduced the loneliness families feel when they are the only members of their group housed, and it eliminated the levelling sanction of jealous kin and the problems created when relatives still on the road use the dwelling as a gathering place. Moreover, when a family's kinfolk are also housed, it is less likely that the family will leave its home and return to the road in response to some problem or conflict.

In both areas, an effort was made to place the families who did the most scavenging in houses with large backyards or at the end of a block, where they would have room to store their scrap metals. This enabled many men to continue in their regular work patterns. The adjustment process was also facilitated by the efforts of local committee workers to involve the Travellers in the community. Children were encouraged to join the Boy Scouts, Girl Guides, and other social clubs. Adults were encouraged to attend community activities, and some were assisted in joining local voluntary associations such as the credit union.

CHAPTER EIGHT

Summary
and Conclusions

This study has focused on the economic and social adaptations Irish Tinkers have made to their new urban environment following the breakdown of their former rural way of life. The salient points of the study are summarized in this section; the final section draws some conclusions about the nature of the Travellers' urban adaptation and about the adaptive process of poor, marginal groups in general.

The traditional economic niche of the Tinkers, as well as of other European itinerants, was characterized by the performance of a variety of trades and services. Flexibility was required in that the Travellers' work was dictated by the needs of each individual farmer approached and by the seasonal changes in the agricultural cycle. The limited market or demand for their skills in any one district necessitated itinerancy; this, in turn, shaped other aspects of their adaptation. Travel bands, for example, had to be small and fluid. The need for transportation and shelter on the road called for a special material culture, including tents, carts, wagons, and horses. Because of the Tinkers' nomadism and occasional predatory subsistence activities such as the poaching and pilfering of farm produce, relations between itinerants and the settled population were ambivalent. On the one hand Tinkers were welcomed for the services they performed; on the other hand they were always mistrusted.

Following the Second World War, the rapid modernization of rural Ireland resulted in the obsolescence of most of the Travellers' traditional skills and services. No longer able to make a living in the countryside, large numbers migrated to urban areas.

Migration often occured in stages, first to the nearest provincial towns and then to large urban centers—notably Dublin—and in some cases on to England. In urban areas, the men signed onto the dole and scavenged for scrap metal and an assortment of second-hand goods, and the women begged.

The economic niche of urban Tinkers today is virtually identical to that of the past. Their subsistence activities are still marginal ones requiring both flexibility and mobility, although because of the population density of cities and the motorized transport many Travellers have, it is no longer as necessary for the family unit to change residence. In economic dealings with settled folk, Tinkers also continue to use many of the same exploitative strategies. Because of discrimination on the part of the settled Irish as well as certain subcultural factors, few Travellers have adopted the work patterns of the settled community. Instead, many have become heavily dependent upon State welfare and the charity of private individuals and institutions.

The shortage of appropriate camping locations and the number of itinerants living in urban areas, particularly in Dublin, has forced many families to share camps with Tinkers from territories other than their own. Those living on government sites, which contain up to thirty-nine families, are even more crowded. In these large and heterogeneous camps there is much uncertainty and tension in interpersonal and intergroup relations. Lacking formalized mechanisms for maintaining social control, urban Tinkers have attempted to cope with these conditions in a variety of ways, some more effective than others. Their primary method is simply to maintain social distance from unrelated families and to avoid involvement in any situation which could lead to conflict.

Families are generally secretive and reveal little information about themselves. In such an environment, gossip is an important means of learning about others and about how to deal with them. Developing a reputation for being tough is also important, since the use of force or its threat is a powerful social sanction in itinerant society. Tensions between individuals which cannot be dealt with directly, short of conflict or violence, are often defused in the culturally sanctioned "time out" of the drinking session. When tensions lead to actual conflict, or in response to many other problems, Tinkers physically remove themselves from the problem by shifting to another camp.

Certain conditions of the urban milieu have brought about significant changes in marriage and family patterns. The increased economic power of Traveller women and the modernizing influence of their settled patronesses have strengthened the position of women in the family. The resultant adjustment in sex roles, compounded by other factors, has led to much marital instability. Many women respond to the strain by occasional and temporary desertions. Dating and courtship have become common in large urban camps where adolescent boys and girls come into frequent contact with one another and where parental supervision is difficult. Parents have attempted to cope with this problem and with the increasing delinquency of their adolescent sons by arranging marriages for their children at an earlier age, before they have had a chance to mix with the opposite sex or to become sexually involved.

In the last decade, approximately one-fourth of the itinerant population in Ireland has settled in public housing. The major incentives to settle are the amenities and comforts of housing, the increased educational opportunities for children, the prospect of upward mobility, and, for some, a general dissatisfaction with itinerant life. The adjustments required in settlement are not easy for itinerants, and some families have returned to the road. The difficulties encountered include the extra financial strain of utilities and rent, prejudice and animosity of settled neighbors, isolation from kinsmen with its resulting loneliness, boredom stemming from the inability to change surroundings in the traditional way through travel and shifting, and the loss of familiar pastimes. Despite such obstacles, the experience of housed Travellers in several Irish towns demonstrates that under the proper circumstances those who desire to settle are able to adapt relatively rapidly and painlessly.

The Adaptive Process

Travellers have adapted to changes in their economic and social environment, including the loss of their former trades and the uncertainty and conflict in the urban milieu, by modifying and frequently intensifying traditional behavior patterns. The adaptive responses discussed in Chapters Four, Five and Six are not new;

they are largely found, albeit in altered form, in the traditional culture. Scavenging and begging, the major urban subsistence activities, were part of the economic repertoire of rural Travellers who exploited every social resource available to them. The exploitative strategies used in dealing with urban house-dwellers, such as persistence and techniques of impression management, are continuous with the past. Similarly, Tinkers have coped with the uncertainty, mistrust, and social problems of large camps in the city by intensifying social devices found in the traditional culture. Individual coping responses such as secretiveness, withdrawal from interaction, and excessive drinking, and group responses such as close kin marriages and frequent shifting to avoid conflict are not new; rather, they have assumed greater importance in the city.

Although Travellers have so far been able to cope with the urban environment by making minimal adjustments in their traditional culture, not all these changes have been desirable. Coping responses which satisfy immediate subsistence or social needs may have long-range consequences which are maladaptive or dysfunctional. The occupations Tinkers pursue in urban areas provide one example. Scavenging, begging, and welfare have not only satisfied subsistence needs but have in fact increased the real income and standard of living of many families. Materially, they have never been better off. From this perspective the economic adjustment has been highly successful. But because this adaptation requires a high level of dependency, it has brought about a loss of pride and a lowering of self-esteem among many Travellers. It has led to the demise of the old public stereotype of Tinkers as carefree jacks-of-all-trades; a new image of Travellers as parasites is emerging. Although some house-dwellers sympathize with their plight, the Tinkers' dependency has increased the antagonism of some settled folk toward them. Moreover, because Traveller women are the principal recipients of charity in urban areas, they have in many instances displaced their husbands as family breadwinners. This has led to intense marital conflict, and many men have responded to their weakened role in the family by resorting increasingly to physical force as a means of reasserting their masculinity, and to drinking as an escape from the reality of their present situation. Both of these responses, among other factors, further erode marital stability.

It is important to note that responses designed to help people cope with a certain set of social or environmental conditions may also indirectly contribute to those conditions: there is "feedback." Adaptive responses such as drinking and shifting not only have negative side or long-range effects, but may also contribute to the circumstances they were intended to deal with. Shifting, for example, enables Tinkers to escape conflict arising from tensions endemic to large camps, but at the same time it contributes to the uncertainty and tensions by prohibiting long-term associations on which reciprocity and trust are built.

Why then have Travellers adapted in these ways? Part of the answer lies in the tendency of most cultures when confronted with a new environment to turn first to familiar patterns and sanctioned behavioral alternatives (cf. Firth 1951; Nimmo 1972). Most cultures are inherently conservative; people change only enough to meet immediate new demands. Truly innovative change occurs only when the preferred traditional patterns and culturally sanctioned alternatives no longer work. It is at this point that people must look for new models.

Such truisms, however, reveal little about the adaptation of Tinkers and other marginals who are markedly conservative. As economic and social marginals, Travellers simply lack the resources and opportunity structure necessary to develop more innovative and, in the long range, more satisfactory responses to their environment. Employment is a case in point. If Travellers were able to obtain and keep conventional jobs in the settled community, many of the problems which currently confront them would be eradicated or minimized, including the low self-esteem men experience as a result of their economic dependence on settled society and, in many cases, on their wives. Moreover, boredom resulting from idleness, which is caused by the loss of traditional trades and pursuits, might well be eliminated with employment. But because of prejudices against Tinkers and their lack of the requisites of urban life such as literacy, job opportunities are severely limited. As Goulet (1971) notes of Gypsies, "They are the last to be hired and the first to be fired."

Because Travellers are unable to correct basic social inequities or to alter the constraints that perpetuate their relative deprivation and their stigmatized status, they must tolerate and cope with existing circumstances as best they can. Parents, for example, cope with illicit dating and possible promiscuity among daughters and delinquency among sons by arranging marriages at an earlier age. Similarly, urban Travellers respond to the mistrust and ambivalence they feel toward unrelated and unfamiliar kin groups and the increasing instability of marriage by arranging matches for their children with close kinsmen they know and trust.

Many of the coping responses made by Tinkers are aimed primarily at lessening the immediate anxiety and psychic pain created by their new environment. The excessive consumption of alcohol among men is one obvious example. Similarly, the decision to shift to a new camp is usually motivated by a desire to escape or avoid interpersonal conflict, boredom, or some other personal problem rather than to confront the factors underlying it.

In a context in which resources and opportunities are severely limited, such fatalism and resignation to one's basic circumstances is itself a coping response. As Friedland and Nelkin note in their study of migrant laborers in the United States:

> The adaptive response to the disorganized circumstances of migrant life is apathy and escapism. This response does not indicate that the migrants have different values nor does it imply that their behavior is pathological or deviant . . . . Rather, such behavior is consonant with the needs and definitions imposed by their social context. Although some patterns appear disorganized, they serve in fact to make life viable under conditions of uncertainty, ambiguity, and dependence (1971:2).

Parker and Kleiner (1970) have demonstrated convincingly the adaptive significance of a fatalistic approach to life in another resource-poor environment. In their study of low-income Blacks in Philadelphia, they found that individuals who had high mobility aspirations (those who were most intent on forging a better adaptation) suffered higher rates of mental illness than individuals who passively or fatalistically accepted their position.

At present, housing within the settled community offers an escape from many of the constraints under which Tinkers live. It is obvious that the desire of many Travellers to be housed is based upon a wish to escape the limitations and problems associated with Traveller life today. For only when Travellers have settled and gained some degree of acceptance from the settled community will many of the job and educational opportunities of settled folk be available to them. Although the social and personal adjustments required by housing are great, the experience of housed families in Mullingar and Tuam has shown that under the right circumstances itinerants can adapt to housing with little difficulty. The rapid success achieved by these families who have been exposed to a new opportunity structure demonstrates forcefully that behavior is to a large degree shaped by the socioeconomic environment in which people live.

Bibliography

BOOKS AND ARTICLES

Adams, Barbara, et al.
 1975 *Gypsies and Government Policy.* London: Heinemann.

Allport, G.W.
 1954 *The Nature of Prejudice.* Boston: The Beacon Press.

Anonymous
 1937 "Meanderings: Our Irish Gypsies—the Tinkers." *Ireland's Own*, 17 April, p. 4.

Arensberg, Conrad, and Kimball, Solon
 1940 *Family and Community in Ireland.* Cambridge, Massachusetts: Harvard University Press.

Arnold, Fredrick S.
 1898 "Our Old Poets and the Tinkers." *Journal of American Folklore* 11:210-20.

Balikci, Asen
 1968 "Bad Friends." *Human Organization* 27:191-99.

Barth, Fredrik
 1955 "The Social Organization of a Pariah Group in Norway." *Norveg* 5:126-43.

————.
 1969 *Ethnic Groups and Boundaries.* Boston: Little, Brown and Company.

Bennett, John
 1969 *Northern Plainsmen: Adaptive Strategy and Agrarian Life.* Chicago: Aldine.

Blom, Jan-Petter
    1969   "Ethnic and Cultural Differentiation." In *Ethnic Groups and Boundaries,* Ed. Fredrik Barth, pp. 74-85. Boston: Little, Brown and Company.

Blood, Robert O., and Wolfe, Donald
    1960   *Husbands and Wives: The Dynamics of Married Living.* New York: Free Press.

Braroe, Niels W.
    1965   "Reciprocal Exploitation in an Indian-White Community." *Southwestern Journal of Anthropology* 21:166.

Brody, Hugh
    1974   *Inishkillane: Change and Decline in the West of Ireland.* New York: Schocken.

Caudill, Harry
    1962   *Night Comes to the Cumberlands: A Biography of a Depressed Area.* Boston: Little, Brown and Company.

Central Statistics Office
    1971   *Statistical Abstract of Ireland, 1969.* Dublin: The Stationery Office.

Clébert, Jean-Paul
    1967   *The Gypsies.* London: Penguin Books.

Clifford, Sigerson
    1951   *Travelling Tinkers.* Dublin: Dolman Press.

Commission on Itinerancy
    1963   *Report of the Commission on Itinerancy.* Dublin: The Stationery Office.

Connell, K.H.
    1968   *Irish Peasant Society: Four Historical Essays.* Oxford: Clarendon Press.

Crawford, M.H., and Gmelch, George
    1974   "The Human Biology of the Irish Tinkers: Demography, Ethnohistory and Genetics." *Social Biology* 21:321-31.

Cullen, Louis M.
    1968   *Life in Ireland.* London: B.T. Batsford.

DeVos, George, and Wagatsuma, Hiroshi
 1966 *Japan's Invisible Race: Caste in Culture and Personality.*
 Berkeley: University of California Press.

Eames, Edwin, and Goode, Judith
 1973 *Urban Poverty in a Cross-Cultural Context.* New York:
 The Free Press.

Evans, E.E.
 1957 *Irish Folk Ways.* London: Routledge and Kegan Paul.

Fenner, Frank and Ratcliffe, F.N.
 1965 *Myxomatosis.* Cambridge: Cambridge University Press.

Firth, Raymond
 1951 *Elements of Social Organization.* London: Watts.

Fortes, Meyer
 1953 "The Structure of Unilineal Descent Groups. *American
 Anthropologist* 55:17-41.

Foster, George
 1967 *Tzintzuntzan: Mexican Peasants in a Changing World.*
 Boston: Little, Brown and Company.

_____, and Robert Kemper
 1974 *Anthropologists in Cities.* Boston: Little, Brown and Company.

Freeman, T.W.
 1972 *Ireland.* London: Methuen and Company.

Friedland, William H., and Nelkin, Dorothy
 1971 *Migrant: Agricultural Workers in America's Northeast.*
 New York: Holt, Rinehart and Winston.

Garabino, Merwyn
 1971 "Life in the City: Chicago." In *The American Indian in
 Urban Society,* Eds. Jack Waddell and Michael Watson,
 pp. 168-205. Boston: Little, Brown and Company.

Glazer, Nathan
 1975 "The Culture of Poverty: The View from New York City"
 In *City Ways: A Selective Reader in Urban Anthropology.*
 Eds. John Friedl and Noel Chrissman, pp. 402-15. Boston:
 Little, Brown and Company.

Gluckman, Max
    1963   "Gossip and Scandal." *Current Anthropology* 4:307-16.

Gmelch, George
    1975   "The Effect of Economic Change on Irish Traveller Sex Roles and Marriage Patterns." In *Gypsies, Tinkers and other Travellers,* Ed. Farnham Rehfisch, pp. 257-69. London: Academic Press.

Gmelch, Sharon Bohn
    1975   *Tinkers and Travellers.* Dublin: The O'Brien Press.

——————, and Gmelch, George
    1974   "The Itinerant Settlement Movement: Its Policies and Effects on Irish Travellers." *Studies: An Irish Quarterly Review* 68:1-16.

——————.
    in press   "The Emergence of an Ethnic Group: The Irish Tinkers." *Anthropological Quarterly.*

Goffman, Erving
    1959   *The Presentation of Self in Everyday Life* New York: Doubleday.

——————.
    1963   *Stigma: Notes on the Management of Spoiled Identity.* Englewood Cliffs, New Jersey: Prentice Hall.

Goulet, Denis A.
    1971   *The Cruel Choice: A New Concept in the Theory of Development.* New York: Atheneum.

Graburn, Nelson
    1969   *Eskimos without Igloos: Economic and Social Development in Sugluk.* Boston: Little, Brown and Company.

Graves, Theodore
    1971   "Drinking and Drunkenness among Urban Indians." In *The American Indian in Urban Society,* Eds. Jack Waddell and Michael Watson, pp. 274-311. Boston: Little, Brown and Company.

Gray, Tony
    1966   *The Irish Answer: An Anatomy of Ireland.* London: Heinemann.

Hamasy, Louise
    1959   "Changing Women's Roles and Economic Development."
          American Anthropologist 59:101-11.

Hannan, Damian
    1970   *The Rural Exodus.* London: Chapman Press.

Harper, Jared
    1973   "Irish Traveller Cant in Its Social Setting." *Southern Folk-
          lore Quarterly* 37:101-14.

——————, and Hudson, Charles
    1971   "Irish Traveller Cant." *Journal of English Linguistics* 15:78-86.

Heymowski, Adam
    1969   *Swedish Travellers and Their Ancestry: A Social Isolate or
          an Ethnic Minority.* Uppsala: Almquist and Wiksells
          Boktryckeri.

Honigman, John
    1968   "Interpersonal Relations in Atomistic Communities." *Human
          Organization* 27:220-29.

Humphreys, Alexander J.
    1966   *The New Dubliners.* New York: Fordham University Press.

Irish Folklore Commission
    1952a "Toradh Geistiuchain ar Na Tinceiri." ("Tinkers Questionnaire")
          Volume 1255. Unpublished material in the archives of the
          Department of Folklore, University College, Dublin.

——————.
    1952b "Toradh Geistiuchain ar Na Tinceiri." ("Tinkers Questionnaire")
          Volume 1256. [1]

Jacobsen, David
    1971   "Mobility, Continuity, and Urban Social Organization." *Man*
          6(4):630-45.

——————.
    1973   *Itinerant Townsmen: Friendship and Social Order in Urban
          Uganda.* Menlo Park: Cummings Publishing Company.

[1](Additional information on Tinkers is found in volumes 619, 815, 925, 1037, 1195, 1218, 1358, and 1387.)

Kennedy, Robert
    1973   *The Irish: Emigration, Marriage and Fertility.* Berkeley: University of California Press.

Kessel, Neil, and Walton, Henry
    1965   *Alcoholism.* London: Penguin Books

Leland, Charles G.
    1891   "Shelta." *Journal of the Gypsy Lore Society* (first series) 2:321-3.

LeVine, Robert
    1965   "Sex Roles and Economic Change in Africa." *Ethnology* 5:186-93.

Liebow, Elliott
    1967   *Tally's Corner: A Study of Negro Street Corner Men.* Boston: Little, Brown and Company.

Macalister, Stewart
    1937   *The Secret Languages of Ireland,* pp. 130-282. Cambridge: Cambridge University Press.

MacAndrew, Craig, and Edgerton, Robert
    1969   *Drunken Comportment, A Social Explanation.* Chicago: Aldine.

McEgill, Sherley
    1934   "The Tinker and the Caravan." *Irish Press*, 3 March, p. 8.

McGrath, Sean
    1955   Miscellaneous information on Tinkers, particularly in County Clare. Volume 1391, pp. 3-40, and volume 1436, pp. 1-10, 22-30. Unpublished material in the archives of the Department of Folklore, University College, Dublin.

MacGreine, Padraig
    1931   "Irish Tinkers or 'Travellers'." *Bealoideas: Journal of the Folklore Society of Ireland* 3:170-86.

————.
    1934   "Some Notes on Tinkers and Their 'Cant'." *Bealoideas* 4:259-63.

MacMahon, Brian
    1967   *The Honey Spike.* Dublin: Bodley Head.

MacRitchie, David
 1889 "Irish Tinkers and Their Language." *Journal of the Gypsy Lore Society* 1:350-7.

Meenan, James
 1970 *The Irish Economy Since 1922.* Liverpool: Liverpool University Press.

Meggers, Betty
 1971 *Amazonia: Man and Culture in Counterfeit Paradise.* Chicago: Aldine.

Messenger, John C.
 1969 *Inis Beag: Isle of Ireland.* New York: Holt, Rinehart and Winston.

Meyer, Kuno
 1891 "On the Irish Origin and the Age of Shelta." *Journal of the Gypsy Lore Society* (first series) 2:257-66.

Miller, Walter B.
 1965 "Focal Concerns of Lower-class Culture." In *Poverty in America,* Ed. Louis A. Ferman, pp. 396-405. Ann Arbor: University of Michigan Press.

Nelkin, Dorothy
 1969 "A Response to Marginality: The Case of Migrant Farm Workers." *British Journal of Sociology,* pp. 375-89.

————————.
 1970 "Unpredictability and Life Style in a Migrant Labor Camp." *Social Problems* 17:472-86.

Nimmo, H. Arlo
 1972 *The Sea People of Sulu.* San Francisco : Chandler.

Orme, A.R.
 1970 *Ireland.* Chicago: Aldine.

Parker, Seymour, and Kleiner, Robert
 1970 "The Culture of Poverty: An Adjustive Dimension." *American Anthropologist* 72:516-27.

Quinn, David Beers
 1966 *The Elizabethans and the Irish.* Ithaca, New York: Cornell University Press.

Radcliffe-Brown, A.R.
    1952   *Structure and Function in Primitive Society.* New York: Free Press.

Rehfisch, Farnham
    1958   "The Tinkers of Perthshire and Aberdeenshire." M.A. thesis in the Library of the School of Scottish Studies, Edinburgh.

——————.
    1961   "Marriage and the Elementary Family among the Scottish Tinkers." *Scottish Studies* 5:121-47.

——————, ed.
    1975   *Gypsies, Tinkers and Other Travellers.* London: Academic Press.

Rubel, Arthur, and Kupferer, Harriet
    1968   "Perspectives on the Atomistic Type Society." *Human Organization* 27:189-90.

Sampson, John
    1891   "Tinkers and Their Talk." *Journal of the Gypsy Lore Society* (first series) 2:204-21.

Schoor, Alvin L.
    1970   "Housing and Its Effects." In *Neighborhood, City, and Metropolis,* Eds. Robert Gutman and David Popenoe, pp. 709-29. New York: Random House.

Shibutani, Tamotsu, and Kian, Kwan
    1965   *Ethnic Stratification: A Comparative Approach.* New York: Macmillan and Company.

Simson, Walter
    1865   *A History of the Gypsies.* London: Samson Lowe and Son and Marston.

Stephens, James
    1914   *The Demi-Gods.* London: Macmillan and Company.

Stephens, William
    1963   *The Family in Cross-Cultural Perspective.* New York: Holt, Rinehart and Winston.

Sutherland, Anne
    1975   "The American Rom: A Case of Economic Adaptation."
            In *Gypsies. Tinkers and Other Travellers,* Ed. F. Rehfisch.
            pp. 1-39. London: Academic Press.

Synge, John M.
    1907   *The Tinkers Wedding.* Dublin: Maunsel and Company.

——————.

    1912   *In Wicklow and West Kerry.* Dublin: Maunsel and Company.

Szwed, John
    1966   *Private Cultures and Public Imagery: Interpersonal Relations*
            in a Newfoundland Peasant Society. St. John's, Newfound-
            land: Institute of Social and Economic Research.

Turnbull, Colin
    1968   "The Importance of Flux in Two Hunting Societies." In
            Man the Hunter, Eds. Richard B. Lee and Irven Devore,
            pp. 132-37. Chicago: Aldine.

Turner, John
    1970   "Barriers and Channels for Housing Development in Modern-
            izing Countries." In *Peasants in Cities,* Ed. William Mangin,
            pp. 1-19. Boston: Houghton-Mifflin.

Valentine, Charles
    1968   *Culture and Poverty: A Critique and Counterproposals.*
            Chicago: University of Chicago Press.

Walsh, Brendan M.
    1970   "Marriage Rates and Population Pressure: Ireland 1871 and
            1911." *Economic History Review* 23:148-62.

Yoors, Jan
    1967   *The Gypsies.* New York: Simon and Schuster.

Index

adaptation, definition of *5–6*
Adams, Barbara , et al. *82*
alcohol consumption *10, 85–86,*
    99, 101–105, 107, 116, 121–
    122, 147
Allport, G. W. *37*
Arensberg, Conrad *17, 19, 95,*
    123
Arnold, Frederick *9*
atomistic society *91–92*

Balikci, Asen *91*
Barth, Fredrik *25, 34, 36*
begging *19–20, 45, 72–79,*
    145–146, 149
Bennett, John *5, 6*
Blom, Jan-Petter *36*
Blood, Robert *113*
boredom *103–104, 109, 148*
Braroe, Niels *66*

camps (*see also* sites)
    conditions of *28, 55–57,*
        59, 106
    location of *28, 53–60*
    size of *28, 55, 58, 91*
    rural *28*
    urban *48, 54–58, 106, 109*
carts, flat *25–26*
Caudill, Harry *88–89*
Central Statistics Office *43–44,*
    49, 53, 130
charities *52–53, 105*

children *74, 96–97, 99–100,*
    128–129, 141
chimney sweeping *17*
Clébert, Jean-Paul *21, 25, 34*
Clifford, Sigerson *103*
Commission on Itinerancy
        establishment of *51*
        Report of *4, 19, 21, 26,*
            28, 31, 50–52, 128
conflict *99, 107–108*
        faction fights *33*
        husband-wife *116, 118–*
            125, 128, 132–133
        interpersonal *99, 107–108*
        mother-in-law *123–124*
        with settled Irish *22, 34–*
            37, 140–141
conflict resolution *32, 98–99,*
    107–109, 122, 124–125, 127,
    132
Connell, K. H. *10*
consumption patterns/material
    goods *85–87, 144, 152*
courtship *125–129*
Crawford, M. H. *117, 130*
crime *16, 21, 24, 36, 101–102,*
    109, 128

death *33, 108, 148*
delinquency *109, 128*
dependency (*see* welfare)
DeVos, George *37*
discrimination/prejudice *35–37,*
    50, 138, 140–141

drinking (*see* alcohol consumption)
Dublin
    Corporation *55, 58*
    County Council *58*
    population of *53*
dwellings/shelter *25–27, 58–60,
   137, 140*

Eames, Edwin *6*
ecological orientation *5–6*
economic change/breakdown
   42–46, 87–89, 157–158
economic niche *13–14, 25,
   87–89, 157–158*
economy/occupations *16–22,
   45–47, 63–85, 87–89, 145–
   146, 154*
education *108, 151*
emigration to England *49–50,
   109*
employment (*see* wage labor)

fairs *16–17, 33*
family planning *81, 117–118*
Famine, the Great *9*
farm labor *18–19, 43–44*
fatalism *162*
Fenner, Frank *45*
Firth, Raymond *161*
Flynn, Michael *131, 138*
Fortes, Meyer *32*
fortune telling *20–21*
Foster, George *100*
Friedland, William *162*

Galway City *53, 141*
Garabino, Merwyn *121*
gift-giving *97–101*
gladar box *24*
Glazar, Nathan *89*
Gluckman, Max *97–98*
Goffman, Erving *73*

gossip *97, 110*
Goulet, Denis *153, 161*
Graburn, Nelson *128*
Graves, Theodore *104–105*
Gray, Tony *45*
Gypsies *21–22, 26, 28, 30, 34,
   36, 82–83, 144, 153*

Harper, Jared *37*
Heymowski, Adam *25, 34*
Holylands *7, 91, 94, 98, 106,
   108–109, 119–122*
Honigman, John *91*
horses *16–17, 26, 43, 60–61,
   145*
horse dealing *16–17, 43*
housing (*see* settlement)
Housing Act of 1931 *137–138*
Humphreys, Alexander *123*
hunting *21–22*

illegitimacy *10, 127*
illiteracy (*see* literacy)
infant mortality *117*
interpersonal relations *92, 94–
   101, 102–105, 107–108, 147*
income *78, 85–86, 114*
Ireland
    east-west differences *22, 24,
      144*
    map *23*
    population *49, 53*
    settlement pattern *14*
Irish Folklore Commission (I.F.C.)
   13, 33, 35, 73
integration (*see also* passing)
   138, 143, 149, 151
itinerancy (*see* travel)
Itinerant Settlement Committee
   (ISC)
    history of *51*
    organization/work *50–53,
      59, 61, 94, 129–130,
      144, 149, 154*

policies *51–53, 129–130,
    139, 149*
questionnaire *8, 107, 144*

Jacobsen, David *110*
jealousy *120–121, 147*
joking behavior *98–99, 103*

Kennedy, Robert *44*
Kessel, Neil *104*
kinship *32, 93, 95–96, 107, 147*
    clan *32*
    lineage *32–34, 131–132*
    residence pattern *32, 122*

Labre Park *58–59, 106, 109*
levelling tendency/levelling
    mechanisms *84, 99–101, 147*
LeVine, Robert *113*
Liebow, Elliott *122*
literacy *82*
loneliness/isolation *146–147, 153*

MacGreine, Padraig *24–25, 38,
    119, 125*
Macalister, Stewart *37–38*
MacMahon, Brian *28, 103*
MacRitchie, David *125–126*
marriage *115, 120, 124–134*
    age at *128–130*
    close-kin *130–134*
    "match" *115, 126–127,
        132*
    settled Irish *130*
McAndrew, Craig *102*
mechanization, agricultural
    42–45
Meenan, James *42, 44*
Meggers, Betty *5*
Meyer, Kuno *37*
migration
    causes of *41–46*
    settled Irish *48–49, 138*

to Dublin *47–49*
    to provincial towns *46–49*
Miller, Walter *99*
Moate *141*
mother-son ties *123–124*
motorization *65, 87, 158*
Mullingar *46, 131, 150–154*

Nelkin, Dorothy *100*
Nimmo, Arlo *161*
Norwegian Taters *3, 25, 28, 34,
    36*

Orme, A. R. *14*
outcast status *35–37, 103*

Parker, Seymour *162*
passing *143–144*
patroness-client relationships
    75, 116–117
pawning *87*
peddling *17, 19, 45*
police (*gardai*) *30, 38, 92, 108–
    109, 115, 132*
poteen 10
premarital sex *125, 127–128*
present-time orientation *145*

Quinn, David *10*

rabbits
    myxomatosis *44*
    snaring *21–22*
Radcliffe-Brown, A. R. *98*
Rehfisch, Farnham *34, 126, 132*
Repairs Grant Scheme *150*
research methods *7–8*
roadside trading *71–72*
Rubell, Arthur *92*

Sampson, John *21, 25, 37–38*
scavenging *47, 63–72, 145*
Schoor, Alvin *143, 147*
Scottish Tinkers *34, 126, 132*
scrap metal merchants *68–70*
secrecy *95*
sedentarization (*see also*
    settlement) *47, 105–106*
self-esteem/self-image *103–104,
    116, 143, 161*
separation, marital *124–125,
    132–133*
settlement/housing
        adaptation to *145–154,
            159, 163*
        attitudes, settled Irish
            140–141, 152
        government grants for *150*
        history of *137–138, 149*
        motivative factors in
            141–143
        obstacles to *145–148*
        statistics *137, 140*
Settlement News 52
sex roles *113–122*
Shelta/Gammon *10, 37–39, 66*
Shibutani, Tamatsu *153*
shifting (*see also* travel) *88, 105–
    110, 127, 147–148*
sites, official (*see also* camps)
    58–60, 92, 106, 142
        opposition to *140*
social control *32, 91–94, 104,
    107, 133*
social resources, definition of
    5, 6
spalpeens 9
St. Mel's Terrace *138, 148–149*
Stephens, James *28, 103*
Stephens, William *114, 118*
stereotypes, Tinkers *36, 74,
    103, 153*
Sutherland, Anne *82–83*
swindling *16, 24, 66–69*

Synge, John M. *103*
Szwed, John *97*

tents *4, 25–26*
tigins 58–60, 92–93
Tinkers/Travellers
        census *50, 117, 137*
        early history *8–10*
        identity *83, 103, 143*
        relations with settled Irish
            *22, 24, 30, 34–39, 60–
            61, 66–67, 103, 116,
            138–140, 146–147,
            149–150, 153*
tinsmithing *14–16, 42–43*
toughness *99*
travel/itinerancy (*see also* shifting)
        circuits/routes *28–30*
        difficulties in *142*
        distance *30*
        group size *31–32*
        modes of *25–30*
Tuam *46, 148–150, 153–154*
turf/peat *44*
Turner, John *152*

uncertainty
        causes of *91–94, 110*
        managing *94–100, 107–
            110, 131–133*

Valentine, Charles *6*

wage labor *82–85, 151, 161*
wagons, barrel-top *25–27*
welfare/dependency *46–47,
    80–82, 83, 88–89, 117, 126,
    160*
wife-swapping *114*

Yoors, Jan *28*